CLANDESTINE
PARACHUTES
PICK-UP OPERATIONS

Jean-Louis PERQUIN

Histoire & Collections

CONTENTS

Mont Valérien : « Action », a high relief by Alfred Janniot : Free France keeps on fighting while holding to her breasts her sons who died fighting for the survival of the fatherland.

3

On 21st September 1942, during a BBC radio broadcast called « Les Français parlent aux Français » (the French speak to the French) at 20 : 25 hours, the speaker said :

« …during two years, Pierre Brossolette has led the struggle of the Fighting French on the front of the interior. Pierre Brossolette is in London. Pierre Brossolette is now talking to you… »

« Close to you, among you, without you even knowing anything about them, men are fighting the enemy. Killed, wounded, executed, tortured, hunted down, often cut from their families, fighters that are all the more moving since they have no uniforms, no standards ; they belong to regiments without colours that will never see their battle honours ever written in golden letters on shimmering silk; they will only live in the fraternal and torn memory of those who will survive ; French people, salute them. Glory is like those ships on which you not only die under the bright sky but also in the darkness of the coal bunkers. This is how the men of the underground struggle for France fight and die.

French people, salute them ! They are the drudges of glory ! »

Parachute drops and Pick-ups:
How it all started

Above.
Para drop from a Halifax
(Now it can be told, 1946)

1. « Pick-up » is the term normally used to describe a clandestine landing in enemy-occupied territory to insert or exfiltrate agents.

This second book in the « Résistance » series is dedicated to the air liaison operations in support of the Résistance. Divided in two different parts, this work presents the genesis of special air operations, the airplanes, agents training, the different types of markings, the Pick-ups[1], some specific operations, air to ground radio communication systems, the S-Phone and the Eureka beacon. The second part will deal with operations from North Africa, the arrival of American forces and the day para drop operations carried out during the Summer of 1944.

This first part will present the technics and procedures as well as the equipment used to carry out those operations. At this stage, it is important to emphasise the fact that all services and their associated Résistance movement were not born equal. Only the British Services owned the huge assets necessary to support such an undertaking… everything belonged to the British Services and like a very apt French saying goes, « who pays choses the music ». The Free French BCRA (Bureau Central de Renseignements et d'Action) was completely reliant on its British

allies and its commander, Colonel Passy pointed out in his memoires that the Résistance movements in France depended on the British Services like a deep-sea diver depended on its oxygen supply (Part II, page 150). The French requests came after the IS and SOE requests and were then subjected to aircraft availability, weather (both in the UK and in France) and finally moon phases as pilots and navigators required enough light to find their way to the intended DZs. Finally, when the relationship between General de Gaulle, the leader of the Free French and the British Prime Minister Winston Churchill was strained, the availability of British support tended to be seriously affected even though it never was totally cut off. On that subject, Passy wrote: « whatever the political difficulties between our leaders, we rarely found a closed door at the British secret services and this was even truer with the OSS. » (Part II, page 141). Thus, when dealing with BCRA operations, it is important not to mix up the capability to set a reception committee for a para drop or a Pick-up and the number of operations that really were carried out.

THE GENESIS OF SPECIAL AIR OPERATIONS
The First Word War, the beginnings

IN 1933, in the foreword of a book dedicated to these Missions, General Denain wrote presciently : « *In the future, should any new war be declared, the same missions would then be accomplished as a normal task and on a large scale. These missions would not be called « special » anymore, as they would get their own resources, large and combined, and would become genuine joint expeditions. Entire units will land in enemy-held territory to drop or*

Pick-up sizeable detachments from all arms and services meant to accomplish large reconnaissance or destruction expeditions as well as frontal or reverse attacks. All this is not within the realm of the imagination. It is the truth to which anyone has to get prepared, whether to use it, or to guard against it. »

The infiltrations and Pick-ups of agents

Agents drops and Pick-ups operations behind enemy lines appeared as soon as armed forces started operating air assets .

Even if they remained secret for a long time, their existence was brought to light by the publication of a research document by the French Army Service des Etapes (the service in charge of supply depots along the main routes) on the 23rd of July, 1918. These pick-up operations, known then as Special Missions, consisted in dropping agents in order to carry out intelligence gathering missions, and sometimes sabotage. Few Pick-ups were made, the agents having to rely on personal initiative to return to France accross Netherlands via Belgium. There were

Top left.
Italian balloonist.

Top right.
French balloonist. Notice the reserve parachute in its conical box.

Ci-contre.
A German observer jumps from a balloon 1916.
(Robert Lenoir collection)

many custom officers among these agents. They used to go on mission with a box filled with a dozen carrier pigeons and with compromisingly large amounts of money!

In total, more than sixty French agents were dropped by air by forty pilots among whom Guynemer, an ace with 54 aerial victories. The first drop was performed on the 18th of November, 1914, South of Catelet near Peronne with an aircraft flown by Second Lieutenant Pinsard. These missions, that became of high importance, saw their peaks on the 23rd of September 1915, when 12 missions were simultaneously executed, dropping 12 agents behind enemy lines during an offensive in the Champagne region.

At the end of the conflict, the very first agents were parachuted behind enemy lines. These drops were done at an altitude of 1,000 metres so that the aircrafts would remain inaudible from the ground. Balloon crew parachutes were used by adapting them under the cabin of the aircraft.

The British, the Italian and the Germans also used this new type of air warfare.

The parachute also allowed the intelligence services to insert agents behind enemy lines, preventing pilots from having to perform dangerous landings. The Italian agents were the first to carry out operational jumps. In the autumn of 1918, as it was preparing its offensive in

the Veneto region, the Italian high command requested information about the Austrian forces. Major Dupont, Head of the Italian Army Special Services, decided it was the right time to drop his agents. He recruited and trained three officers coming from Veneto: Lieutenant Tandura jumped during the night of the 9th to 10th of August 1918 with a cage containing the pigeons that would enable him to report his intelligence finds; Lieutenant Nicoloso jumped in September, Lieutenant Barnaba shortly after. These three "paratroopers" officers contributed to the victory of Vittorio Veneto in October 1918 and received the Gold Medal for Military Valour.

Above.
Jean Ors, one of the first parachutists ever to be dropped is seen here in position before take off in a plane piloted by Mr. Lemoine.
(SHD Air)

Top left.
In 1890, Kate Paulus was the first woman ever to fold her own parachute. She did over 150 jumps and died aged 67 in 1935. The filiation leading to the A Type parachute is obvious.

Right.
German balloonist. Notice the reserve parachute in its round box.
(Robert Lenoir collection)

The Second World War, when it all came together

FROM THE BEGINNING OF THE WAR, in 1940, the problem of infiltrating and picking-up sabotage or intelligence agents behind enemy lines arose again. In July 1940, a first intelligence agent, Hubert Moreau, was infiltrated by sea in support of the British Intelligence Service. He was quickly followed by Jack Mansion[1] on the 17th of July as well as by two French Lieutenants from the BCRA (Bureau Central de Renseignements et d'Action or Central Bureau of Intelligence and Operations), Maurice Duclos[2] "Saint Jacques" and Alexandre Beresnikoff "Corvisard" who were dropped 3 km off Saint Aubin in Normandy, on the 4th of August.

On the 21st of August 1940, a special squadron (419 Squadron) was created within the RAF in support of the

1. Compagnon de la Libération by a 7 March 1945 decree.
2. Compagnon de la Libération by a 25 May 1943 decree.

Below.
Painting depicting an observer jumping from a blazing balloon.
(Roger Lenoir collection)

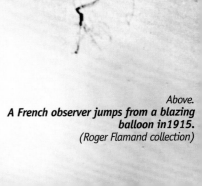

Above.
A French observer jumps from a blazing balloon in 1915.
(Roger Flamand collection)

Secret Intelligence Service (SIS). Later the same month, a first parachute drop was carried out near Paris on behalf of the SIS.

Then, missions were carried out one after the other: Philip Schneidau alias Philipson had to be dropped by a Whitley bomber but bad weather prevented it on five different occasions! The pilot of his aircraft received the following order: "Take this man away and don't bring him back." Philip finally jumped during the night of the 9th to 10th of October 1940, near Montigny, on the edge of the Fontainebleau forest. He was picked-up during the night of the 19th to the 20th of October by a Lysander piloted by Captain W.J. Farley.

Weathered in once again, Farley finally got the clearance to take off to pick Philip up. He left from Tangmere under heavy rain. As the sliding roof of the rear cockpit had been removed to facilitate the speedy boarding of the agent, the rain flooded the rear compartment and rendered the radio unserviceable. Farley found the field South of Fontainebleau, and as expected, Philip turned on the lights that were shaped as an inverted L (This system, drawn by Farley on a restaurant tablecloth, was used for Pick-ups by Lysander and never changed throughout the war).

Farley finally landed and stopped at the first light. Philip climbed into the rear cockpit using the fixed ladder and Farley took off. After the take-off, he noticed that something was interfering with the elevator (one of the controle surfaces). A bullet had passed through the compass situated between Farley's knees. The weather deteriorated again, he now had to fly blind with no compass...the radio was too wet to function and in the open rear cockpit the temperature was icy cold and they were utterly lost. In spite of the bad weather and the fear of veering off course towards Belgium or Holland, they persevered. At around 06:30 hours, Farley reported that the fuel tanks were empty, and around 06:50 hours the engine shut down for good. They glided to the ground. Philip removed all his civilian clothes as they thought they may land in enemy occupied territory. Naked, he jumped from the wreck of the Lysander and ran away, shouting "Wally, come out! It's going to catch fire." But Farley did not move and said, "If there's one thing that will not happen it is that this thing catches fire as there is not a drop of bloody fuel left!". In fact, they had landed in Scotland. This is how, on the 20th of October 1940, the first operation of clandestine pick-up of the Second World War ended.

From then on, around 1,750 agents [3] were to be infiltrated in France by parachute drops.

Above.
A Norwegian parachutist under a Type X parachute.
(Norwegian Armed Forces Museum, Oslo)

Right.
Philippe Schneidau in London.
(MoD)

3. According to the researches carried out by the author over the course of the past twenty years.

« Each month, during the full moon, some «Lysander» or «Hudson», piloted by agents specialized in these courageous performances, would land on chosen landing strips. Men who, each time, put their lives on the line, ensured the marking, the reception or the exfiltration of passengers and equipment, the protection of everything and everyone».

(Charles de Gaulle : War Memories - Volume I, The Appeal)

138 Squadron

Above.
138 Squadron badge: the sword undoes the ties that bind Freedom: Motto: « For Freedom ».

Below.
RAF Tempsford pictured in 2009 ; what is left of a taxiway.
(J-L Perquin)

THE SQUADRON was originally scheduled to be operational in November 1917. After numerous changes of equipment and training, it was officially formed on the 30th of September 1918 and its deployment planned for November, but as the Armistice was signed, it did not have time to reach France. The unit was disbanded on 1st of February 1919.

On the 21st of August, 1940, it was decided to create a special squadron in support of the SIS (419 Squadron). The squadron was reformed on the 25th of August, 1941 when 419 Squadron was renamed 138 Squadron and based at Newmarket. It was tasked with dropping agents, ammunition and equipment inside occupied Europe when using Whitley bombers, and dropping and picking up agents when using Lysanders. At the very beginning, it was composed of six Whitleys and two Lysanders divided into two Flights, "A" Flight specializing in parachuting and "B" Flight in clandestine landings.

In October 1941, the Whitleys were replaced by specially equipped Halifaxes: the front and top turrets were disarmed and removed, oxygen supply equipments were also removed (they were useless at the relatively low altitude used on operation) and a wind deflector was added near the « Joe hole ».

In February 1941, only 161 Squadron was in charge of Pick-up missions with the Lysander.

In March 1942, the squadron moved to what would become its base for the rest of the war: Tempsford. Stirling bombers were delivered in June 1944 and replaced the Halifax from August. Then, the squadron carried out drops in support of resistance movements throughout Europe, from Poland to the Balkans. Following the progress of Allied armies towards Germany, the clandestine missions became less numerous and 138 Squadron was transferred to the Bomber Command on the 9th of March, 1945. Moved to Tuddenham, the squadron was re-equipped with Lancaster and carried out bombing operations until the end of the war.

Above.
Tangmere, 1943 : Flying-officer J. A. Mc Cairns, Squadron-leader Hugh Verity, Group-captain p. c. Pickard, flight-lieutenants P. E. Vaughan-Fowler and F. E. Rymillis.
(Jean-Michel Rémy collection)

Top right.
161 Squadron badge : an open handcuff and a motto : « Set free » in latin

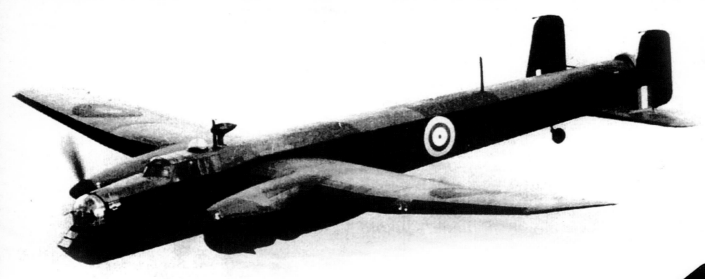

Above.
Withley in flight.

Right.
Wellington in flight.
(Josiane Somers collection)

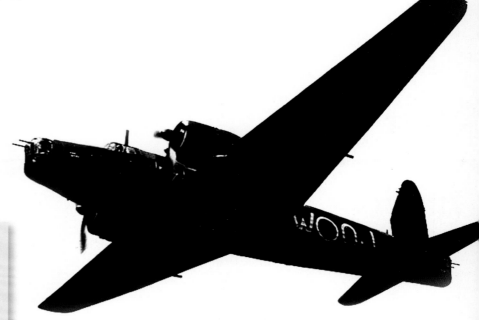

Code letters given to 138 Squadron

WO	From April 1939 to September 1939
NF	From August 1941 to March 1945 and from April 1947 to September 1950
AC	From March 1945 to April 1947

Losses : a total of 135 aircrafts were lost.

138 SQUADRON

AIRCRAFTS	SORTIES	LOSSES	PERCENTAGE
Halifax	1 788	47	2,6 %
Stirling	503	10	2 %
Lysander	64	11	17 %
Hudson	219	1	0,45 %
Whitley	1		
Total	2 575	69	2,7 %
From March to May : Lancaster	105	1	1 %

Determining the exact number of operations carried out by 138 Squadron was not possible due to the lack of figures at the beginning of the conflicts. However, it is known that 438 missions were operated in support of the Resistance, or 2,578 sorties. (Estimates from Captain Batchelor's Group from the RAF)

161 Squadron

Above.
***June 1942,
Wing-Commander Edward
Fielden and the officers
of 161 Squadron.***
(Josiane Somers collection)

Right.
***138 Squadron Short
Stirling in Tempsford
in 1944.***
*(Jean-Michel Rémy
collection)*

THIS SQUADRON WAS SUPPOSED to have been ready for employment during the First World War, but the conflict ran its course before its activation. The squadron was finally formed in Newmarket on the 15th of February 1942, also incorporating the Royal Flight. It was immediately tasked with the same missions as 138 Squadron : droping agents, weapons and equipment and carry out Pick-ups in support of resistance movements throughout occupied Europe.

In April, it moved to Tempsford with 138 Squadron. Initially three types of airplanes were used: Lysanders, Whitleys and Havocs. The use of the Whitley was discontinued in December 1942, as the Halifax slowly started to replace them from the previous month ; the Havocs were also withdrawn in December 1943. For pick-up missions, some Hudsons arrived in October 1943. The Halifax was replaced by Stirling IIIs and IV in September 1944. The Squadron was disbanded on the 2nd of June 1945.

161 SQUADRON

AIRCRAFTS	SORTIES	LOSSES	PERCENTAGE
Halifax	786	17	2,2 %
Stirling	379	6	1,6 %
Lysander	266	10	3,8 %
Hudson	179	10	5,6 %
Whitley	139	6	4,3 %
Total	1 749	49	2,8 %

The figures are known for sure. It fact, the number of sorties and losses are probably higher. (Estimates from the Captain Batchelor's Group from the RAF)

Above.
161 Squadron's Lysander MA J Jimmy Criquet.

Below.
**RAF Tempsford in1945, Gibraltar Farm were the agents
got ready before jumping into occupied territory.**
(Josiane Somers collection)

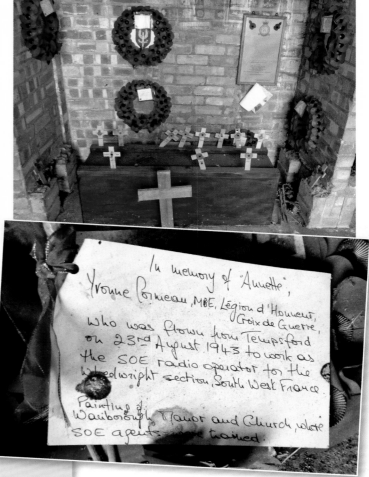

Top and right .
RAF Tempsford in 2009: inside Gibraltar Farm, some flowers and notes in memory of Yvonne Cormeau a.k.a « Annette », an SOE F Wheelwright network radio operator who was parachuted during the night of the 22nd to the 23rd of August 1943 near Bordeaux. After having accomplished her mission, she returned to London at the end of the Summer of 1944.
(J-L Perquin)

In memory of "Annette".
Yvonne Cormeau, MBE, Légion d'Honneur,
Croix de Guerre,
who was flown from Tempsford
on 23rd August 1943 to work as
the SOE radio operator for the
Wheelwright section, South West France.

Painting of
Wanborough Manor and Church, where
SOE agents were trained.

Code letters given to 161 Squadron

AX	from April 1939 to September 1939
MA	from February 1942 to 1945
JR	from April 1944 to 1945 (for Lysander only)

Losses:
- 13 Lysander :
  4 aircrafts shot down in mission over France ;
  4 aircrafts lost in France (mishaps on landings) ;
  3 aircrafts crashed because of the fog on returning to England ;
  2 aircrafts bogged down on landing, burnt on site.
Of the 13 pilots, 7 survived those accidents and 6 were killed.

- Hudson : no loss, only 2 aircrafts bogged down but ultimately recovered.

S OPERATED BY
SQUADRONS

*Norwegian paratroopers bringing CLE « Paratroops »
containers to a Whitleys. It is possible to see on
that picture that those parachutists wear the British
« Jacket, Parachutist ».*
(Norwegian Armed Forces Museum, Oslo)

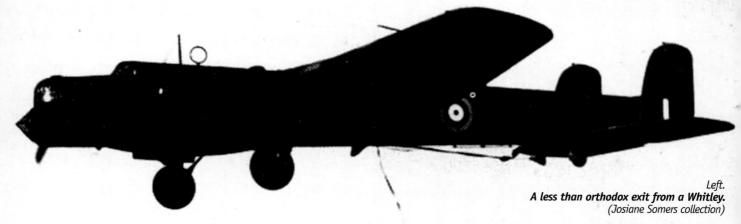

The Amstrong Whitworth Whitley AW 38

The Whitely was a British bomber designed in 1934. It did its maiden flight on 17th March 1936. 1,814 Whitley were built before production stopped in July 1943.

Wing span: 25.6 m
Length: 21.08 to 21.48 m depending on the type
Height: 4,57 m
Maximum take off weight: 15,200 kg
Bomb load: 2,500 kg
Top speed: 400 kph at 5,000 m
Range: 3,600 km
Crew: typically five

This was the airplane used for the first experiments and the first missions.

On 19th June 1940, when the British armed forces activated N°1 Parachute Training School in Ringway (Manchester), 6 Whitleys Mk II bombers were alloted to this training establishment. The square shape of the Whitley tail could accomodate ten men. The tail gunner position could be used as a platform as well as the powered retractable two-gun ventral "dustbin" turret

which could be fitted with two swing doors. The first trials were carried out in July: two instructors jumped by the rear platform and six by the ventral position. The ventral hatch was considered the best option even though it was dangerous since five of the ten parachutists had to jump facing the wind, leading to possible malfunctions in the opening of the parachute canopy.

The Whitleys during the first operations

Operation Colossus (February 1941): on February 7, 1941, in order to destroy the Tragino bridge and aquaduct in Italy, thus depriving the Brindisi, Bari and Foggia harbours and industrial estates of water, 38 men (or 39, accounts vary) of X Platoon, 11 SAS Battalion (the former No 2 Commando) left Malta onboard 51 and 78 Squadron aircrafts and, overflying France, headed for Luqa in Malta where they landed on a bomb-cratered airstrip on February 8.

The raid was launched during the night of the 9th to the 10th of February. Seven officers and 28 paratroopers under the orders of Major Pritchard were split between six Whitleys. Each Withley was also loaded with six containers. Two other Whitleys were loaded with bombs in order to carry out a deception bombardment on Foggia, 45 km away from the aquaduct. In the end, five Whitley managed to drop their human cargo near the target area

but the sixth aircraft, which had gotten lost, dropped its paratroopers in a nearby valley. All the equipment containers were not dropped as some of the releasing mechanism had frozen. One of the Whitley which had been tasked with the bombardment of Foggia, T4167, crashed because of an engine failure. Having only suffered limited damages, the bridge was quickly repaired. The raiding party and the crew of the crashed Whitley were taken Prisoners of War (POWs) as HMS Triumph, the submarine which had been tasked with the recovery of the raiders, did not show up as expected.

Opération Savannah (May 1941): based on a proposal made by Capitaine Bergé, and with Général de Gaulle's agreement, a 30-odd man strong Free French paratroopers unit was created in September 1940 in Kent. In November 1940, it was transfered to Ringway. The unit was soon tasked with the attack of a bus transporting German aircrew members belonging to KG 100 on the road between

Top.
Para drop from a Whitley.
(Jean-Michel Rémy collection)

Above.
Withley in flight.
(Josiane Somers collection)

Vannes and Meucon in Brittany. These German airmen were the pathfinders leading the night bombardment raids over the United Kingdom. On 14 May 1941, four men, (sous-lieutenant Petit-Laurent, sergent-chef Forman, sergent Le Tac and caporal-chef Renault) boarded a Whitley captained by Flying Officer (F/O) Oettle, 419 Flight Special Duties (SD). Owing to reduced visibility, the paratroopers (and two containers) were released too late thus landing 8 km away from the intended DZ (Drop Zone). To make matter worse, the German bus has changed its itinerary and the intelligence on which the mission had been built was found to be outdated. The mission was a failure.

Operation Biting (February 1942): the seizure of a complete Wurzburg Radar Station on the Bruneval cliff in the Seine-Maritime département of France by British paratroopers. In January 1942, Lord Louis Mountbatten planned a raid by the 1st Airborne Division in order to seize this Radar. On 15 February, 6 officers and 113 other ranks performed their first training jump for that mission. On the evening of February 27, in Thruxton, Hampshire, they boarded 12 Whitleys Mk V belonging to 51 Squadron. W/Cdr Pickard headed the formation. Soon after having crossed the French coast, Major Frost paratroopers jumped, landing in the snow, about a kilometre away from a villa located very close to the Radar station. The Radar station

Left.
25 May 1941 demonstration jumps from a Whitley.
(Jean Sassi collection)

Below.
SOE dry suit for water jumps.
(Jean-Michel Rémy collection)

he was shot down over Belgium and taken POW with the rest of his crew. A new Whitley, belonging to 78 Squadron, was provided to 419 Flight but it was destroyed in a landing accident. By the end of March 1941, and in order to avoid confusion with the newly created 419 RCAF Squadron, 419 Flight became 1419 Flight. On 25 August, 1419 Flight then became 138 Squadron with a complement of 10 Whitleys.

Many missions were to follow: the longest recorded mission ever carried out by a Whitley was performed by Whitley Z9158 (F/O Hockey–P/O Wilkin) during the night of the 3rd to the 4th of October 1941. The bomber took off from Tangmere in order to drop a Czech radio operator by the name of Frantisek Pavelka in Pardubice, Czechoslovakia. The total duration of the flight was eleven hours and twenty five minutes. During the night of the 27th to the 28th of December 1941, a Whitley did a bombardment mission in Denmark and soon after dropped three agents. One of the parachutes never opened. By the middle of the year 1942, the SOE had lost contact with the Danish underground which wanted to avoid German retaliations on the civilian population. The SOE then decided to drop its agents over water and Morgans Hammers was dropped by a Whitley during the night of the 18th to the 19th of October 1942 over the straits closing the Baltic Sea. In France, several para drops were also carried out over lakes.

In December 1941, 138 Squadron had 12 Whitleys in its inventory. In February 1942, 161 Squadron was activated in Newmarket. Five Whitleys were alloted to its B Flight. In the Spring, the two Squadrons were co-located in Tempsford, Bedfordshire. During the night of the 1st to the 2nd of April 1942, a Whitley (Ft/Sgt Peterson) carried out the first 161 Squadron operational mission (codename « Mackerel ») and dropped three Free French BCRA agents in France. During the night of the 22nd to the 23rd of November 1942, one of the five 161 Squadron Whitley was lost over Belgium. This airplane (S/n Z6629–code MA-N) was to be the last of the 19 Whitley lost in 1942. Three Lysanders and eight Halifaxes were also lost on that year. 161 Squadron flew the last Whitley mission on 22 February 1943 operating a 502 Squadron (Coastal Command) aircraft.

was secured, the most interesting parts of the Radar were dismantled and made ready for the return trip. Meanwhile, Lieutenant Charteris' party, which had been given the task of securing the beach, took longer than expected to accomplish its mission since it had been dropped too far away from its intended target area. Nevertheless, once the mission was completed, the paratroopers still managed to extract as scheduled with Royal Navy landing crafts even though the Operation cost them one KIA and seven POWs.

Special Missions

On 21 August 1940, 419 Flight Special Duties was activated in order to ferry agents into occupied territories. This Flight, under the command of Flight Lieutnant (F/Lt) Farley was to be equipped with two Whitleys and four Lysanders. From August to December 1940, the Whitleys carried out 10 missions: 4 in France, 4 in Belgium and 2 in Holland.

During the night of 14 to 15 February 1941, 419 Flight's new CO, F/Lt Keast (who had taken over from F/Lt Farley, who had been wounded while flying a Hawker Hurricane) took three Polish agents to Cracow, Poland, during an eleven hours and twenty minutes long flight. During the night of 17 to 18 February, while flying Whitley T4264,

The Whitley and the French Resistance.

As early as August 1940, a first para drop was carried out close to Paris in support of the Intelligence Service. Other missions followed in quick succession: on the 9th of Octobre, Philippe Schneidau a.k.a Philipson jumped close to Montigny on the outskirts of the Fontainebleau forest.

In November, in one of a very few such instances, an agent who was supposed to jump close to Morlaix refused to leave the aircraft. In December, two other French agents were dropped near Rambouillet, again in support of Intelligence Service activities: Claude Lamirault a.k.a « Fitzroy » and Jacques Voyer. Jacques Voyer did several jumps into occupied France in order to carry out reconnaissance and sabotage missions. He operated in Corsica, in Vichy

in December 1941 and then again during the night of the 10th to the 11th of April 1944 near Ruffec le Château, 8 km from Le Blanc in the Indre département. Head of the « Vitrail » Sussex mission in Chartes, he was arrested on 10 June 1944. Hit by two bullets, he was nevertheless tortured for more than two weeks (the Nazis sawed his teeth off…) but still he refused to talk. He was shot on 27 June 1944.

The first F section mission took place on 5 May 1941 under the codename of Operation « Bombproof ». During this Operation, in support of the SOE F / Ventriloquist network, S/Ldr Knowles dropped Pierre Bégué a.k.a « Georges », a radio operator, in Vatan near Valençay, 17 km North of Châteauroux. Five days latter, following a radio message from Bégué and in support of the SOE F/Autogiro network, Knowles dropped Pierre de Vomécourt a.k.a « Lucas » and Louis Lefrou de la Colonge a.k.a « Bernard », in the same region but 8 km away from the intended DZ. On the return trip, Knowles'rear gunner managed to shoot down a German Me 110 over Le Mans.

During the night of the 12th to the 13th of June 1941, Sergeant Austin dropped an equipment container close to Limoges near a château belonging to Philippe de Vomécourt, Pierre's brother. During the night of the 8th to the 9th of July 1941, the « Torture » mission of the BCRA (SOE RF) was dropped from a Whitley captained by S/Ldr Knowles. Henri Labit a.k.a « Tab » and Jean-Louis Cartigny a.k.a « Tab W », his radio operator, were tasked with a sabotage mission on the Caen-Carpiquet airbase. J.L. Cartigny was captured and executed. Henri Labit (then only 21 of age) made it to Toulouse where he organised the « Fabuleux » network. Parachuted into occupied France for a second time in May 1942, Henri Labit choose to swallow his cyanide pill when he was arrested on the demarcation line in April 1943.

Georges Bégué and Max Hymans a.k.a « Frederic » were the first to set up a para drop of agents with landing lights and a reception comitee. This Operation was carried out during the night of the 10th to the 11th of October 1941 in the lieu-dit Puyauderie in Saint Jean d'Eyraud between the towns of Périgueux and Bergerac in South-West France. A first BBC message was broadcasted in order to confirm the impeding drop: « Gabriel vous envoie ses amitiés » (« Best regards from Gabriel » which went on the air for the first time on the 2nd of October). On 10 October, a variation in the text of the message, (« Gabriel va bien » or « Gabriel is doing fine »), indicated that the operation was planned for the coming night: the same message was broadcasted again at 13 : 00, 20 : 00 and 21 : 15 hours. The reception commitee, composed of Jean-Pierre Bloch a.k.a « Gabriel », of Doctor Dupuy, the mayor of Villamblard and of Albert Rigoulet, a local mechanic, then got into action. A large cross made of white paper was emplaced on the ground, two lights indicating East and one indicating West were switched on. On its first pass, the Withley dropped three agents, three containers, two radio sets and two millions French Francs in bank notes. The agents, who all belonged to the « Corsican », SOE F network had jumped in the following order: Captaine Clément Jumeau a.k.a « Robert » (died in captivity on 26th March 1944 during a second mission in Germany).; Captain Jack Hayes a.k.a « Eric »; and the radio operator, Lieutenant Jean Le Harivel a.k.a « Hiccup ». The trio was arrested less that ten days after its parachute insertion.

Following the first pass, the ground team had switched the lights off thinking the drop was finished. Deprived of any ground references, the Withley had to drop Daniel Tuberville a.k.a « Diviner » and his two equipment packets and two containers close to Issac, some kilometres away. Tuberville was quiclky arrested but managed to

escape through Spain and ultimately returned to London 28 April 1943.

During the night of the 13th to the 14th of October 1941, Squadron Leader Murphy parachuted Lieutenant Forman (it was his third mission) and René Périou a.k.a « Cadoux » his radio operator in La Martinette close to Fonsorbes (near Toulouse). The plan was to support Henri Labit to prepare Operation « Mainmast » which was scheduled for the night of the 1st of January 1942. René Périou was to be arrested by the Vichy police on 14 May 1942 and deported. By the end of 1942, no less than 70 agents had been inserted into occupied France…

On 2 January 1942 at 03 : 30 hours, Sergeant Jones, flying onboard a 138 Squadron Whitley which had taken off from Saint- Eval dispatched Jean Moulin a.k.a « Max », Raymond Fassin a.k.a « Sif » and Hervé Monjaret a.k.a « Sif W » his radio operator on Eygalières in the Alpilles region (South-East of France). When the Whitley returned to Saint-Eval, it had completed an eleven hours and fifty seven minutes long mission!

This parachute insertion had been quite eventful and on 7 March 1942, Raymond Fassin sent a message to London listing what had gone wrong during that night. Three main causes were given for their various problems:
– *The drop altitude, which was over 500 metres, was too*

Norwegian parachutists jumping from a Whitley.
(NHM Oslo)

Above left.
Jean Moulin.

Above center.
Raymond Fassin,
in Lille in 1943.

Above right.
Hervé Monjaret.
(GCD collection
www.memorialjeanmoulin.fr)

high and it resulted in the agents being scattered over a vast area. This made regrouping even more problematic because of the many hedges criss-crossing the area.

— We were dispatched too late, at 0330 hours, which forced us to bury our parachutes and radio sets in a hurry: this resulted in two parachutes being discovered in the next 15 days.

— We were dropped 15 km from the intended area. The itinerary and advices of Rex and Bruno have not been followed at all. The area is marshy. Rex nearly drowned and he needed more than an hour to extricate himself. We had to do a 25 km daylight route march together.

The task of Jean Moulin was to unify and rally the different Résistance movements. He also had been tasked by Général de Gaulle to create a secret army with a clear delineation between the political and the military branches. He did a return trip to London in order to report on the progresses of his mission. During his visit, Général de Gaulle awarded him the Croix de la Libération. He was picked up from France by a Lysander during the night of the 13th to the 14th of February 1943 using the« Léontine » strip near Ruffey/Seille, North West of Lons le Saunier in the East of France (Operation Porpoise Prawn Gurnard). Jean Moulin then returned to his homeland during the night of the 19th to the 20th of March again by Lysander pick-up to a strip located in Saint Yan, North of Roanne (Operation « Sirène 2 »).

Jean Moulin was arrested on 21st June 1943 in Caluire near Lyons. Horribly tortured, he still refused to talk. Following the failure of his tormentors to break him, he was transferred to Germany but, on the 8th of July 1943, in a train between Metz and Franckfürt, his body broken but his spirit intact, he passed away.

During the night of the 15th to the 16th of June 1943, Raymond Fassin returned to the United Kingdom during Operation « Knuckle-Duster ». He was picked up by a Hudson piloted by Hugh Verity from the « Marguerite » strip located near Feillens, North of Macon. Tasked with a new mission, he was to be parachuted for a second time into occupied France during the night of the 15th to the 16th of September 1943 on the « Chemineau » DZ near Luxerois, 6 km from Is-sur-Tille. Arrested in Paris on the 2nd of April 1944, Raymond Fassin was sent to Germany, to the Neuengamme concentration camp where he died on 12 February 1945.

Hervé Monjaret a.k.a « Sif W » was tasked by Rex to establish liaison with the Franc-Tireur Résistance movement. After two narrow escapes, he finally was arrested by the German police on Sunday the 4th of April, 1943 after the Gestapo had set up a trap specifically for him in Lyons. After several weeks in prison and many hours of brutal interrogation during which he managed to remain mute and in spite of a wealth of evidence against him, he was transferred to the Fresnes prison in Paris, then, on 21 September 1943 to Germany, first to Sarrebrück, then Mauthausen to finally end up in a labour camp in Vienna. He was repatriated to France on 4 May 1945.

On 4 March 1942, a Whitley piloted by Pilot Officer Anderle dropped three NKVD agents in France. Their task was to control the various Communist organisations in the country. Among the agents was Anna Frolova a.k.a Francine Fromont, a.k.a Annette Fauberge, the first ever woman to be dropped into occupied France. The other two agents were Grigory Rodionov a.k.a George Robigot and Ivan Danilov a.k.a Pierre Dandin. The missions continued in 1942 and by the beginning of 1943, Halifaxes were replacing Whitleys.

The Westland Lysander Mk III A

THE LYSANDER was a British army co-operation and liaison aircraft which did its maiden flight on 15 June 1936. The first Lysanders entered service in June 1938 and a total of 1,789 were built. The Mk III version was powered by a 870 hp Bristol Mercury XX radial piston engine

Manufacturer: Westland
Length: 30 ft 6 in (9.29 m)
Wingspan: 50 ft 0 in (15.24 m)
Wing area: 260 ft (24.2 m)
Height: 14 ft 6 in (4.42 m)
Empty weight: 4,365 lb (1,984 kg)
Max. takeoff weight: 6,330 lb (2,877 kg)
Top Speed: 336 kph
Ceiling: 21,500 ft (6,550 m)
Range: 600 miles (960 km)
Armament: 4.303 machineguns

This instantly recognizable aircraft has become the symbol of Pick-up missions. It was the most commonly used airframe for the insertion and Pick-up of spies and agents, especially members of the Special Operations Executive or of the French Résistance. Originating from a 1934 Air Ministry programme which requested an aircraft capable of operating from very short airfields, it became an instant success with its crews. Its main qualities were its high wing, its sturdy landing gear and its exceptional short-field performance. In order to better answer the needs of special operations, a Special Duties (Lysander MK III SD) version was produced. It carried under the fuselage a 570 litres Handley Page Harrow fuel tank which gave the SD version no less than eight hours flying time with four passengers. That sort of feat was not advertised in the training manual and was only performed on return trips from France

The original variable pitch proppeler was soon changed for a Blenheim fixed pitch proppeler. The ladder located

Above.
Lysander 2442.
(Josiane Somers collection)

Right.
The pilot cockpit of the Lysander kept in the Hendon RAF museum.
(J-L Perquin)

on the rear left of the fuselage was designed to facilitate the access to the rear cockpit. The rugs were daubed with a fluorescent paint while the underside of the aircraft was painted flat black. The original 1133/1134 radio set was replaced by a 1154/1155 set which was less bulky.

The very last RAF Lysander were withdrawn from service in January 1946. A former 161 Squadron Lysander was donated to France, to the Invalides museum in Paris in remembrance of the combined clandestine operations carried out during the war. The last Lysander to fly operationaly were operated by the Egyptian armed forces in its 1948 war against the state of Israël.

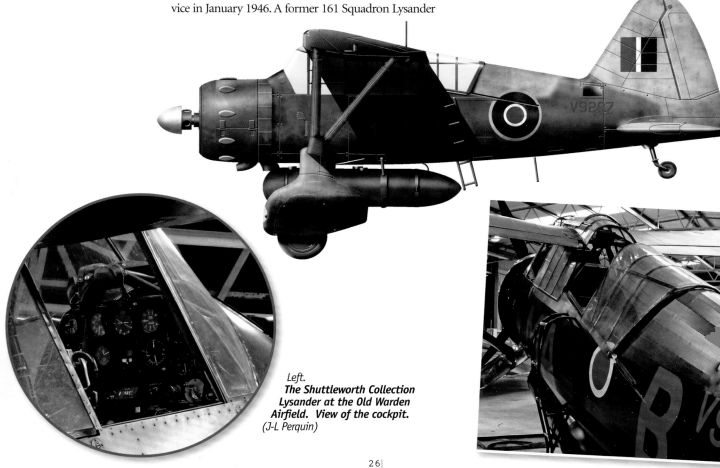

Left.
The Shuttleworth Collection Lysander at the Old Warden Airfield. View of the cockpit.
(J-L Perquin)

The Armstrong Whitworth Albemarle Mk V

Above.
An Albemarle bomber being towed to its hangar.

Right.
Rear view of an Albemarle.

Right bottom.
RAF crew in front of its Albemarle.
(Josiane Somers collection)

Entered service in mid-1942 ; 600 were built. The Albemarles took part in the Sicily, Normandy and Arnhem operations.
Powerplant: 2 × Bristol Hercules XI radial engine, 1,590 hp (1,190 kW) each
Maximum speed: 230 kn (265 mph, 426 km/h) at 10,500 ft (3,200 m)
Cruise speed: 148 kn (170 mph, 274 km/h)
Service ceiling: 18,000 ft (5,486 m)
Range: 1,300 mi (2,092 km)
Wingspan: 77 ft 0 in (23.47 m)
Length: 59 ft 11 in (18.26 m).
Height: 15 ft 7 in (4.75 m)

Wing area: 804 ft² (74.6 m²)
Empty weight: 25,347 lb (10,270 kg)
4 × .303 in (7.7 mm) Browning machine guns in dorsal turret.
Capacity: 10 paratroopers

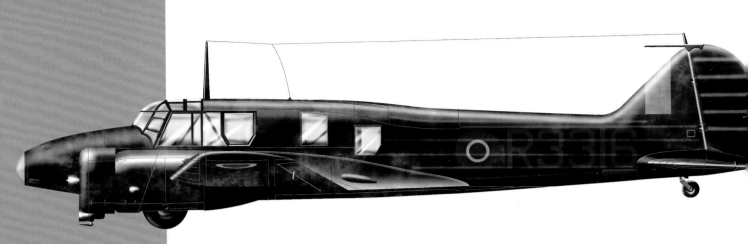

The Avro Anson Mk I

The Avro Anson was a British aircraft from the interwar period. It was the first RAF monoplane with a retractable undercarriage. A distinctive feature of the Anson I was its landing gear retraction mechanism which required no less than 140 turns of the hand crank by the pilot. The Anson was used throughout the war as a reconnaissance airplane and as a trainer for pilots flying multi-engine bombers. From 1941, a 1,822 Mk II version was built in Canada by Federal Aircraft Ltd; deprived of its dorsal turret, powered by two 330 hp Jacobs L-6MB

Below.
Avro Anson in flight.
(Josiane Somers collection)

engines and fitted with hydraulic landing gear retraction rather than the manual system used on the Anson I, the Mk II was partly made of plywood.

Length: 42 ft 3 in (12.88 m)
Wingspan: 56 ft 6 in (17.22 m)
Height: 13 ft 1 in (3.99 m)
Wing area: 463 ft (43.1 m)
Empty weight: 5,512 lb (2,500 kg) Loaded weight: 7,955 lb (3,608 kg) Max. takeoff weight: 8,500 lb (3,900 kg)
Powerplant: 2 Armstrong Siddeley Cheetah IX radial engines, 355 hp each or 2 Jacobs L-6MB de 330 ch (Mk II)
Maximum speed: 188 mph (163 kn, 303 km/h) at 7,000 ft (2,100 m)
Range: 790 mi (690 nmi, 1,300 km)
Service ceiling: 19,000 ft (5,791 m)

The Anson deserves to be in those pages because even though it only did one pick-up it was the first ever to be performed by a twin-engined aircraft in occupied France. Operation Beryl 2 and 3 « Brick » took place during the night of the 1st to the 2nd of March 1942, 1.5 km North East of Segry, close to the town of Issoudun. The crew of the Anson was composed of A.M. Murphy (pilot) and Lieutenant Cossar (navigator). Their task was to recover the pilot and passengers of a Lysander which had crashed on 28 January during Operation « Beryl », namely John Nesbitt-Dufort (pilot), Roger Mitchell a.k.a « Brick », Maurice Duclos a.k.a « Saint Jacques » and Julius Klee-berg a.k.a « Tudor ».

As it had been « borrowed » from the Abingdon Bomber Command training establishment, Anson R 3316 was originally bright yellow but it returned to its home base with a complete coat of black paint…! Rather than face the music, the crew returned it discreetly and parked it safely away from views before making good their escape in a waiting Lysander…

The Vickers-Armstrong Wellington

Above.
**Wellington R 1333
on the ground.**
(Josiane Somers collection)

THIS BRITISH designed twin-engined bomber was built by Vickers-Armstrongs (Aircraft) Ltd. It did its maiden flight on 15 June 1936 and entered service in October 1938. It was withdrawn from RAF service at the end of October 1945. A total of 11,461 Wellington were built between 1936 and 1945.

Crew: 6 (1 pilot, 1 radio operator, 1 navigator/bomb aimer, 1 observer/gunner (nose turret), 1 rear gunner, 1 waist gunner)

Length: 64 ft 7 in (19.68 m)
Wingspan: 86 ft 2 in (26.27 m)
Height: 17 ft 5 in (5.31 m)
Wing area: 840 ft (78.1 m)
Empty weight: 18,556 lb (8,435 kg)
Max. takeoff weight: 28,500 lb (12,955 kg)
Powerplant: 2 Bristol Pegasus Mark XVIII radial engines, 1,055 hp each
Maximum speed: 235 mph (378 km/h) at 15,500 ft (4,730 m)
Range: 2,550 mi (2,217 nmi, 4,106 km)
Service ceiling: 18,000 ft (5,490 m)
Armament
Guns: 6-8 .303 Browning machine guns
Bombs: 4,500 lb (2,041 kg) of bombs

The Wellington was one of the cornerstones of the Bomber Command during the first two years of the war before being superseded by much largers four-engined bombers such as the Avro Lancaster. The Wellington was popularly known as the Wimpy by RAF personnel, after J. Wellington Wimpy from the Popeye cartoons. With Bomber Command, Wellingtons flew 47,409 operations and dropped 41,823 tons of bombs for the loss in action of 1,332 aircraft.

Above.
Wellington « Q VR ».
(Jean-Michel Rémy collection)

Right.
**Wellington BT Z
being refuelled.**
(Josiane Somers collection)

The Handley Page Halifax Type I to IX

THIS BRITISH BOMBER was designed in 1937 by Handley Page and did its maiden flight on 25th October 1939. A total of 6,100 Halifax were built by five different companies.

Crew: 6 or 7 ; a dispatcher could sometimes be added when dropping parachutists .

Length: 71 ft 7 in (21.82 m)

Wingspan: 104 ft 2 in (31.75 m)

Height: 20 ft 9 in (6.32 m)

Wing area: 1,190 ft (110.6 m)

Loaded weight: 54,400 lb (24,675 kg)

Powerplant: 4 Bristol Hercules XVI radial engine, 1,615 hp each

Performance

Maximum speed: 282 mph (454 kph) at 13,500 ft (4,115 m)

Range: 1,860 miles (3,000 km)

Service ceiling: 24,000 ft (7,315 m)

Armament Guns: 8 .303 in (7.7 mm) Browning machine guns (4 in dorsal turret, 4 in tail turret), 1 .303 in (7.7 mm) Vickers K machine gun in nose

Bombs: 13,000 lb (5,897 kg) of bombs

Payload : 7,500 Ibs (3,400 kg) at a range of 1,300 km (800 miles).

Above.
Containers being loaded in the bomb bay of an Halifax.
(Philippe collection)

Ci-contre.
Nose Art of Halifax Yvonne « 9W Y » in Norway.
(Norwegian Armed Forces Museum, Oslo)

ANGELUS DU SOIR.

Dropping speed : 125 mph (200 kph)

Standard load in the cargo drop role: 15 320 Lbs (145 kg) containers, parachutes included.

18 125 lbs (56 kg) packets, parachutes included.

The weight of the packets was limited by the capability of the airframe as well as by the manhandling constraints. If special packets or agents were transported, the payload was limited to 6,800 lbs (3,084 kg) in order to give more room to the agents and to ease the manhandling of the packets by the dispatcher. The Halifax used for para drops were specifically modified ; because they were operating at low altitude, the oxygen system was dispensed with ; the nose and dorsal turrets were also removed and a wind deflector was added in front of the « Joe hole » through which the agents jumped.

Above.
Propaganda leaflet drop by a Halifax.
(Fonds Rivière, CHRD Lyon, J-L Perquin)

Left.
Crashed 138 Squadron Halifax.
(Jean-Michel Rémy collection)

Below.
**138 Squadron Halifax B II, « V-Victor »,
in Fayid, Egypt in Decembre 1942.
During the night of the 28th to the 29th
of December 1941, this plane, piloted by
Flight Lieutenant Ron Hockey dropped
two SOE-trained Czech agents (Jozef
Gabík and Jan Kubiš) to carry out
Operation Anthropoid, the assassination
of the infamous « Butcher of Prague »
SS-Obergruppenführer Reinhardt
Heydrich, which finally took place on
27 May 1942.**
(Jean-Michel Rémy collection)

Top.
Container drop by a Halifax.
(Georges Ricard collection)

Above and left.
**Containers being loaded in the bomb
bay of a Halifax.**
(Now it can be told, 1946)

Top.
138 Squadron Halifax dropping parachutists.
(Now it can be told, 1946)

Libya,1943, Halifax II « FS B » JP246 is a B II Series IA Halifax modified for
the SOE and used in the Mediterranean theatre of operations. This airplane was
posted as missing in action on 8 October 1944 over Brindisi.
(Jean Sassi collection)

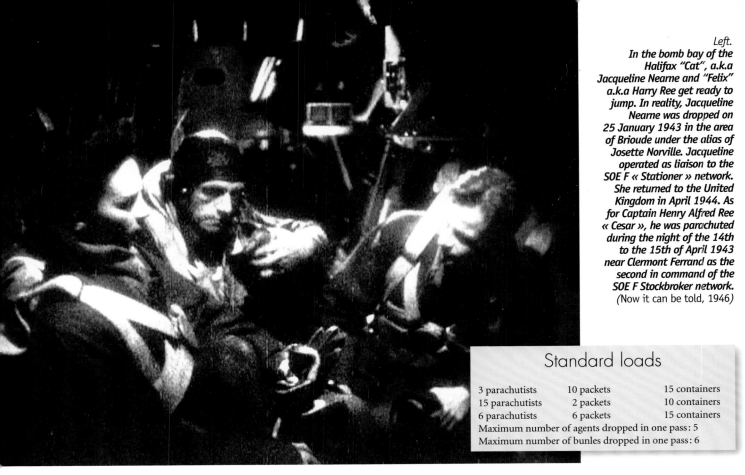

Left.
In the bomb bay of the Halifax "Cat", a.k.a Jacqueline Nearne and "Felix" a.k.a Harry Ree get ready to jump. In reality, Jacqueline Nearne was dropped on 25 January 1943 in the area of Brioude under the alias of Josette Norville. Jacqueline operated as liaison to the SOE F « Stationer » network. She returned to the United Kingdom in April 1944. As for Captain Henry Alfred Ree « Cesar », he was parachuted during the night of the 14th to the 15th of April 1943 near Clermont Ferrand as the second in command of the SOE F Stockbroker network.
(Now it can be told, 1946)

Standard loads

3 parachutists	10 packets	15 containers
15 parachutists	2 packets	10 containers
6 parachutists	6 packets	15 containers

Maximum number of agents dropped in one pass : 5
Maximum number of bunles dropped in one pass : 6

Right.
An interesting view of the hatch used to drop parachutists from in Halifax MK VII NA377 ; this hatch was known as the « Joe Hole ». This particular airplane is the one and only preserved Halifax in the world. Crewed by Tarrant-based Canadian airmen belonging to 644 Squadron, this airplane had just dropped some containers when it was hit by the Flak on 24 April 1945, 75 km North-East of Oslo in Norway. It crashed on a frozen lake and sunk in 200 metres of water. It finally was recovered in 1995 and sent to Canada for restauration. It is now visible in the Trenton Canadian Air Museum.
(Stein Aasland)

Above.
Para drop from a Halifax.
(Now it can be told, 1946)

Below.
August 1945, a Norwegian underground member belonging to D-13 Group (Milorg area) is seated in front of Halifax 9WY. This airplae had only just carried out a demonstration drop on the Gardermoen airfield, near Oslo. Notice the wind deflector for parachute drops on the airplane's undebelly.
(Norwegian Armed Forces Museum collection, Oslo)

The Short Stirling

Above.
**The impressive Short
Stirling on take off.**

THIS BRITISH BOMBER was designed in 1937 and did its maiden flight on 19 September 1938. A total of 2,389 Stirlings were built.

Crew: 8 men
Length: 87 ft 3 in (26.6 m)
Wingspan: 99 ft 1 in (30.2 m)
Height: 28 ft 10 in (8.8 m)

Wing area: 1,322 ft (122.8 m)
Empty weight: 44,000 lb (19,950 kg)
Loaded weight: 59,400 lb (26,940 kg)
Max. takeoff weight: 70,000 lb (31,750 kg)
Powerplant: 4 Bristol Hercules II radial engine, 1,375 hp each.
Maximum speed: 255 mph (410 km/h) at 21,000 ft (6,400 m).
Cruise speed: 200 mph
Range: 2,330 mi (3,750 km) or 1,200 km with 6,500 kg of bombs.
Service ceiling: 16,500 ft (5,030 m)
Bombs: Up to 14,000 lb (6,340 kg) of bombs
Exit speed: 125 mph (200 kph)
Standard load in the cargo drop role: 18 C, H or C.L.E. British 320 Lbs (145 kg) containers, parachutes included, 10 125 lbs. (56 kg) packets, parachutes included.

It was also possible to load containers under the wings of the Stirling, bringing the total load to 24 containers and 10 packets. This aircraft was very well suited to airborne operations, dropping its 15 parachutists three times faster than the time other aircrafts needed to drop five agents.

Left.
« Action Station »; a parachutist ready to jump in a Short Stirling.
(Josiane Somers collection)

Above.
A Short Stirling dropping containers.
(Jean Sassi collection)

Bottom right.
Parachutists exiting Short Stirling "C 5G" through the "Joe hole".
(still from "Carve her name with pride").
(Carve her name with pride, 1958)

Right.
Short Stirling in flight.
(Jean-Michel Rémy collection)

Bottom.
Short Stirling crewmembers.
(Josiane Somers collection)

Standard loads

-	8 packets	18 containers
15 parachutists	3 packets	15 containers

The containers were never dropped at the same time as the agents.
Maximum number of agents dropped in one pass: 5
Maximum number of bunles dropped in one pass: 6

Next page, top.
A Short Stirling dropping containers near Verdun.
(Jean-Michel Rémy collection)

Center and bottom of next page.
30 June 1945, Earls Colne airfield in the UK. Norwegian underground members are given a demonstration on the organisation of para dropping operations by the RAF's 38 Group. On the circled picture, it is possible to notice the winch which was used to hoist containers under the Short Stirling's wings.
(Norwegian Armed Forces Museum collection, Oslo)

The Lockheed Hudson

T HE LOCKHEED HUDSON was an American-built multi-role aircraft initially produced for the RAF. It did its maiden flight on 10 December 1938 and entered service in 1939. A total of 2,936 Hudson were produced until June 1943.

Crew: 3 to 5
Length: 44 ft 4 in (13.51 m)
Wingspan: 65 ft 6 in (19.96 m)

Height: 11 ft 10 in (3.62 m)
Wing area: 551 ft (51.2 m)
Empty weight: 12,000 lb (5,400 kg)
Loaded weight: 17,500 lb (7,930 kg)
Max. takeoff weight: 18,500 lb (8,390 kg)
Powerplant: Pratt and Whitney Twin Wasp R-1830-S3C4-G, 1,200 hp each

Top.
161 Squadron Hudson.
(Now it can be told, 1946)

Right.
Drawing depicting the emplaning of « out » passengers in a Hudson during a pick-up operation in occupied France. The Eureka beacon is on and the security party is in place.
(Pierre Lorain collection)

Maximum speed: 218 kt (246 mph, 397 km/h)
Range: 1,700 nm (1,960 mi, 3,150 km)
Service ceiling: 24,500 ft (7,470 m)

Armament: 2 ".303 in (7.7 mm) Browning machine guns in a dorsal turret, 2 ".303 Browning machine guns in the nose

Bombs: 750 lb (340 kg) of bombs or depth charges

The first Hudson delivered to the RAF was the personal aircraft of King George VI. The crew composition could vary quite extensively, from the basic three (pilot + navigator + radio operator) to four and sometimes even five. The Hudson started being used for special operations from the end of 1942 onwards. To this purpose, a hatch was added on the bottom of the fuselage. The Hudson could carry up to ten passengers in spartan conditions, (suitcases used as seats and back directly against the fuselage). They accessed the rear compartment through a door located on the rear left of the aircraft. Thanks to its range, the Hudson could reach any part of the French territory from its bases in England. For operations over the South of France and during the short Summer nights, Hudson crews had to divert to North African airfields on the other side of the Mediterranean Sea rather than return to their home bases. Much heavier than the Lysander, the Hudson required considerably longer airfields and hard surfaces. From November 1942 until the Liberation, a minimum of 42 Pick-ups were carried out by Hudson.

Top right.
The boarding operations being completed, the members of the reception committee move away from the Hudson before it takes off.
(Now it can be told, 1946)

Below.
Day Pick-up by Hudson in France.
(Jean-Michel Rémy collection)

Chronology and evolution of the establishment by Squadron

Squadron	Date	Type and number of aircrafts
419	21/08/1940	2 Whitley + 2 Lysander
419	September 1940	2 Whitley + 2 Lysander
138	25/08/1941	2 Lysander + 10 Whitley + 3 Halifax + 1 Maryland (experimental)
138	October 1941	2 Lysander + 10 Whitley + 3 Halifax + 1 Wellington
138	February 1942	2 Whitley + 6 Halifax + 1 Wellington
161	February 1942	7 Lysander + 5 Whitley + 2 Wellington + 1 Halifax
138	June 1942	5 Whitley + 12 Halifax
161	June 1942	7 Lysander + 5 Whitley + 2 Wellington + 1 Hudson
138	November 1942	15 Halifax
161	November 1942	5 Halifax + 7 Lysander + 2 Wellington + 1 Hudson
138	08/05/1943	20 Halifax
138/161	Autumn 1943	Temporary reinforcement with Stirlings on loan from Bomber Command
161	01/01/1944	5 Halifax + 10 Lysander + 2 Wellington + 5 Hudson
138	May 1944	22 Stirling
161	May 1944	13 Lysander + 6 Hudson

Training the Agents
The Parachute Course

Stick of Norwegian paratroopers ready to emplane into a Whitley.
(Norwegian Armed Forces Museum, Oslo)

INITIALLY taught by the RAF at the Central Landing Establishment in Ringway (soon to become N° 1 Parachute Training School), the parachute course for special agents quickly became separated from the normal training of conventional paratroopers.

In February 1941, SOE purchased Dunham House in Cheshire which became SOE Ground Training School under the title of Special Training School (STS) 51. Major C.J. Edwards was to be the CO of this school from its activation on 11 March 1941 to its disbandment in August 1945.

In March 1941, in order to increase the output of this school as well as to increase operational security between agents of different nationalities, another training establishment was opened: Fulshaw Hall (STS 51 b). From then on, the school was able to train 50 agents at a time (25 on each training site). A third site was later to be created in York House under the title of STS 51c. Depending on weather conditions, the course lasted five to seven days. After the ground training phase, the agents would do five to seven descents. The norm was then reduced to four descents in order to align it with the armed forces parachute course. After having conducted a mission into occupied France, on their return to the United Kingdom, some agents were given some « refresher training jumps » before heading back again

to France…in October 1942, the SOE started teaching water jumps in dry suits. In 1943, the Leg Bag (also known as the Kit Bag according to some documents) was introduced. All students were taught its use except for Danes and Norwegians as their national commands considered that the use of this equipment could potentialy lead to injuries. The Reception Committee training was also given by STS 51 until the Summer of 1944 when the teaching of all those procedures was centralised at the « Reception Committee School » of Howburry Hall which had been activated in June 1943. In Ringway, the SOE also trained 872 SIS students (including the Sussex mission) and 172 SAS.

Top left and right.
Flight Lieutenant John C.Kilkenny's invention in Ringway: a device meant to reproduce the exit from the Whitley's hatch and the PLF (Parachute Landing Fall).
(Public Archives of Canada)

Previous page, bottom left.
Kilkenny Circus, the slide used to practice Parachute Landing Fall (PLF).
(Public Archives of Canada)

Previous page, bottom right.
Dunham House, STS 51a. The manor of Dunham House was the home of the trainee agents during their parachute course. Close to Tatton Park, the DZ located on Lord Edgerton's estates, Dunham House is located roughly 15 kilometres away from the Ringway Parachute Training School. Called STS 51a by the SOE it was known as STS 33 by the OSS.
(Jack Risler)

Right.
Balloon jump in Tatton Park with a camoufled canopy.
(Aldo Boccone collection)

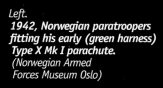

Left.
1942, Norwegian paratroopers
fitting his early (green harness)
Type X Mk I parachute.
(Norwegian Armed
Forces Museum Oslo)

Above left.
1942, Norwegian paratroopers emplaning
into a Whitley. Notice the Jackets
Parachutists and the early Type X
Mk I parachutes (green harness and
camouflaged outer bag)
(Norwegian Armed Forces Museum, Oslo)

Left.
British paratroopers emplane in a Whitley at the Central Landing Establishment in Ringway. Notice the Type X Mk I parachutes. They can be identified by the static line coiled outside the main bag.
(IWM)

1942, This Norwegian paratroopers packs a Lee Enfield rifle in a felt wrapping before placing it inside a CLE « Paratroops » container.
(Norwegian Armed Forces Museum, Oslo)

Below.
1942, Norwegian paratroopers in a Whitley.
(Norwegian Armed Forces Museum, Oslo)

1942, Norwegian paratroopers being dropped from a Whitley.
(Norwegian Armed Forces Museum, Oslo)

Above.
Parachutist Qualification badge. This badge was created by Army Council Instruction (ACI) 1589 dated 28 December 1940. On an army green material backing, it depicts an open parachute embroidered in white flanked by a pair of wings embroidered in light blue. The wings are permanently awarded, even if the holder no longer serves in an airborne unit. This badge has to be worn on the right sleeve, between the shoulder and the elbow. A regulation dated 12 February 1941 stated that the para wings will have to be surrendered if the holder refuses to jump. On 17 June 1942 ACI 1274 added that the para wings would have to be worn on top of all other badges, 2 inches (5 centimetres) from the shoulder. These para wings belonged to Free French SAS Colonel Roger Flamand.
(J-L Perquin, E. Lefebvre collection)

Below.
1942, Norwegian paratroopers ready to jump from a Whitley (« Attention station »). Note the « Step-in » Jackets, Parachutists.
(Norwegian Armed Forces Museum, Oslo)

The parachute drop operation organizer's course

Once the Eureka and S-Phone were operational, it soon became obvious that further training was necessary to prevent any more operator's mistakes and blunders in the field. Centralized training was the best option and thus a new special training school was established.

In September 1943, a manor by the name of Howbury Hall was requisitioned and became STS 40. It fell under the control of C Group. The school itself was under the command of a Major and the training was given by two SOE officers, who taught field procedures for landing strips marking as well as employment of the S-Phone, two RAF officers (one Radar specialist supported by a RAF NCO and a liaison officer to Tempsford) as well as some Signals specialists tasked with the maintenance of

all the radio equipment but who frequently were used as secondary instructors. Basic training lasted about ten days. The first three days were devoted to theoretical studies and to the operation and maintenance of the S-Phone. The next three days were dedicated to Eureka training and to the setting up of a reception committee. A night culmination exercice, complete with a live drop followed during which the trainees had to demonstrate they had mastered the use of those equipment and that they were ready to receive a para drop. On the request of several resistance movements from different nations, a shortened three-day course was organised. It only covered the organisation of a reception committee and did away with S-Phone and Eureka training. On the other hand, all the

SOE torchlight (small type) Reference in the SOE catalogue: H 139
Cylindrical in shape and painted matt black, this torch was fitted with
four filtered lenses (red, yellow, green and blue) as well as a spare 3.5 Volt
bulb in the lid of the rear part. Length: 15.2 cm; diameter of the battery
compartment: 2.5 cm, diameter of the lens: 3.8 cm, weight : 85 grams.
(Musée de l'Ordre de la Libération, Paris)

agents who were supposed to operate those special equipment had to successfully go through the dedicated STS 40 training. This school closed on 28 May 1945.

Program of the 10 day course

Sunday: in-processing, welcome brief by CO STS 40.

Monday 1st day: the whole day was dedicated to the operation of the S-Phone. Four lessons were followed by a series of practical exercises (PE).

Tuesday 2nd day: S-Phone training and, at the end of the day, landing strip marking PE: how to use torchlights and Morse code exercise. The night was dedicated to S-Phone PE

Wednesday 3rd day: S-Phone PE and Morse code with torchlights.

Thursday 4th day: S-Phone and S-Phone batteries maintenance

Friday 5th day: lesson on containers, container drops, container contents and on agent parachute insertion. Visit of a teaching room and theoretical test on the S-Phone.

Saturday 6th day: lesson on DZ selection and pre-drop reconnaissance followed by a sand table exercise.

Sunday 7th day: lesson on aircraft navigation and on the equipment supplied to resistance movements. Training film on the use of the Eureka-Rebecca system. Theoretical lesson on the Eureka and introduction to the Mark IB and II. PE with two sets. Lesson on operational procedure. Introduction to the Mk III, III AM and IIIB followed by PE with those three sets. 19 : 45 hours Preparatory briefing for the coming night's PE: a live reception of a parachute drop. 21 : 30 hours the student designated as the commander of the operation issued his orders.

Rest of the night: live drop PE.

Monday 8th day: Eureka II, III AM and IIIB field training exercises (FTX). Morse code PE. After action review on the previous night's PE.

Tuesday 9th day: maintenance of the Eureka set and batteries. Preparatory briefing for the coming night's PE: a second live reception of a parachute drop. 21 : 30 hours the student designated as the commander of the operation issued his orders. Rest of the night: live drop PE.

Wednesday 10th day: theoretical test on the Eureka and on the organisation and running of reception committees. After action review on the previous night's PE. Final words by the CO. Departure of the students.

Above.
Another still from "Now it can be told ». A group of trainees in a classroom in STS 61. On the blackboard, the instructor is showing the typical landing strip marking.
(Now it can be told, 1946)

Left.
SOE torchlight (large type) with two 1829 batteries. Reference in the SOE catalogue: H 140. Similar in design to the smaller model (H 139), it only differed by its dimensions and by the fact it incorporated an extra filter (ultra-violet). Length: 17,7 cm, diameter of the battery compartment: 3.8 cm, diameter of the lens: 4.4 cm, weight: 127 grams. This torch also was cylindrical in shape and painted matt black.
(B. Barthelot, private collection)

The pick-up operation organizer's course

THIS COURSE was set up in 1941 in answer to the development of Pick-up operations in occupied France. This week-long course was exclusively run by the RAF on the Tempsford airfield, the home base of 161 Squadron. For the course, Tempsford was renamed STS 61. The course concentrated on the selection of appropriate airstrips and associated approach paths and on the management of « in » and « out » passengers. This was a foundation course and pilots would not land on an airstrip which had not been recced and validated by a graduate from this course. The trust between the pilot and the agent on the ground who had selected the landing strip had to be extremly strong as the success of the Pick-up operations depended on it.

Above.
Lysander V 9707 doing a medical evacuation in Vesime Cortemilla (Cueno) in April 1944.
(Aimé Flaba collection)

Below and next page above.
STS 61 training course for reception committees; 161 Squadron's Lysander Mk III SD JR « M » R 9125 (JR : April 1944 to 1945) takes off. This plane is currently on show at the RAF museum in Hendon and is the last remaining 161 Squadron airplane. Unfortunately, it is missing its external long-range tank. The ladder has been repainted in the Army camouflage pattern. On the other hand, the rear cockpit is still in the SD version
(Now it can be told, 1946)

Naval and para-naval operation organizer's course

NAVAL COURSE fall outside the frame of this book but they deserve a passing mention as they were taught in a very similar fashion as the air operations courses. They used a number of identical technical devices such as the S-Phone and, from 1943 onwards, most agents who followed air operations courses would also follow a naval course in order to be able to support the forthcoming Allied advance into occupied territories.

The purpose of the naval course was very similar to the aim of the Pick-up course. On completion, agents had to be able to conduct the reception or extraction of agents or equipment through naval assets. In order to comprehend the importance of those naval operations, suffice to say that the current state of historical researches permit to confirm that during the duration of the conflict around 1,500 personnel were inserted into France by naval operations and another 3,000 picked up; these figures include operations carried out in the Channel, the Atlantic and the Mediterranean Sea. Naval vessels operating this service to France were based in the Helford River and those ferrying personnel and equipment to Norway operated from the Shetland Islands. The training for naval operations was only given by the Naval Section (D/Navy). The para-naval course covered the basics of small boats boarding, boat attacks, target reconnaissance and the management of « in » and « out » passengers and equipment in a maritime environment.

Freedom come from the sky

I was born in a workshop
Assembled by weary hands
Silk gown I won't be
I only want to serve the Paras

In silk canvas I am folded
Soon I will take flight
On a back, like a parasol
To save occupied France

I am a bit of freedom
By men hardly won
Resist, I am here with you!
Victory is before us

This poem, written by the école élémentaire « le clos de la Ferme de Torcy » (Seine & Marne) won the 2008 André Maginot public-spirit and memory prize in the Elementary School category

ELATED EQUIPMENT

Once again, everything had to be started from scratch and lessons drawn from the 1918 parachute drops were used as a starting point.

At this point, the reader has to understand that it is quite difficult to give a precise list of those equipment as they were constantly evolving as reports came back from the field. They also were not destined to be returned once drawn from the stores as the standard operating procedure was to destroy them as soon as the parachute jump was completed. Still, some pieces of equipment have reached us through the years, either because some members of the reception committee took it upon themselves to keep them in spite of the terrible risks they were running or because the speed of the Allied advance of the Summer of 1944 meant that some agents did not have the time or the need to destroy them.

*A Norwegian paratrooper getting ready
to land with a Type X parachute.
(Norwegian Armed Forces Museum Oslo)*

The parachutes

UNTIL 1939, the British armed forces had not seen the need to develop airborne units and thus no specific equipment existed. The only reliable parachute then used by the British forces was the Irvin rescue parachute designed for aircrews. The standard type had a 24 ft. (7.3 m) canopy but the decent rate was still fairly high and it caused frequent injuries. Thus, a larger, 28 ft. (8.5 m) canopy was introduced and used for training jumps. Further development were undertaken and led to the introduction of two new type of parachutes. Type X parachutes were issued to regular airborne units and Type A parachutes were dedicated to special operations.

Above.
British paratroopers emplane in a Whitley at the Central Landing Establishment in Ringway. Notice the Type X Mk I parachutes. They can be identified by the static line coiled outside the main bag.

Left.
Side view of two British paratroopers equipped with a camouflaged Type X Mk I parachute X Mk I. The way the static line is coiled and maintained between two vertical pockets is much in evidence here.
(IWM)

Next page.
Norwegian parachutist fitting his Type X parachute before a training jump. He wears an Oversmock and a Bungey training helmet.
(Norwegian Armed Forces Museum, Oslo)

Type X parachutes

Right.
Outer bag and static line of a Type X Mk I parachute.
(Stein Aasland)

Below.
August 1942. Those paratroopers belonging to the 6th Royal Welsh have just landed on Tatton Park, the Central Landing Establishment DZ in Ringway. Notice the Type X parachutes with camouflaged canopy.
(IWM)

The Ringway-based RAF Central Landing Establishment quickly adopted as the safest system the static line hooked to a single point inside the dropping aircraft and then to an anchor line cable in order to be able to drop several parachutists in quick succession. The parachute opening sequence proposed by James Gregory and Raymond Quilter (of the G.Q. Company) was also adopted. The parachute, carried on the back of the operator, opened in the following manner: inner bag, suspension lines, canopy. Raymond Quilter offered an improvement with an inner bag called « Statichute ». This system, sometimes called « suspension lines first » reduced the risks of parachute incidents by creating a permanent tension between the canopy and the suspension lines and reduced the felt parachute opening shock which was brutal with « canopy first » types of parachutes used until then. Developed in close coordination with the CLS, this parachute was

Rear view of a British paratrooper equipped with a Type X Mk I parachute. The way the static line is coiled and maintained between two vertical pockets is much in evidence here. (IWM)

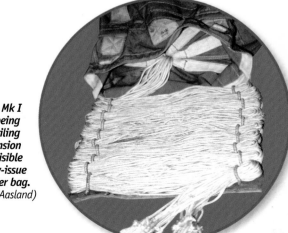

Mannequin of an SOE parachutist equipped for an operational mission. (J-L Perquin)

B.P. PACK, OUTER. Mk. II

6157

REF. No. 15A/503

Above.
Type X Mk II parachute with the early harness. On top of the bag, it is possible to see the « window » which allows the static line to be coiled outside of the bag. This particular parachute was recovered in the South-East of France.

Left.
Label of a Type X Mk II parachute bag found in the South-East of France. (J-L Perquin)

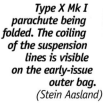

Type X Mk I parachute being folded. The coiling of the suspension lines is visible on the early-issue outer bag. (Stein Aasland)

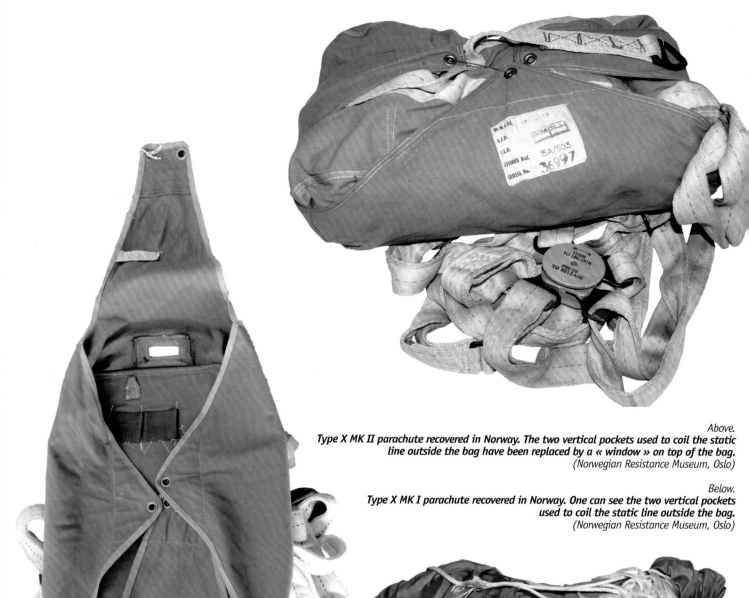

Above.
Type X MK II parachute recovered in Norway. The two vertical pockets used to coil the static line outside the bag have been replaced by a « window » on top of the bag.
(Norwegian Resistance Museum, Oslo)

Below.
Type X MK I parachute recovered in Norway. One can see the two vertical pockets used to coil the static line outside the bag.
(Norwegian Resistance Museum, Oslo)

Type X MK II parachute outer bag in the open position. The « window » for the static line is visible.
(E. Lefebvre collection)

called the Type X MK. I and it was used throughout the Second World War. The diameter of the canopy was 28 ft. (8.5 m) with a 2 ft. (55cm) vented apex and 22'6 (2.38 m) suspension lines.

In order to increase the safety and efficiency of the parachute without changing its general operating principle, some alterations were later made to the Type X. The position and storing of the static line and the folding of the suspension lines led to some changes on both the outer and inner bag and to a new mark, the Type X Mk II. This new system placed the static line on top of the outer bag, limiting the risks of twists in the risers and suspension lines that could prove perilous in the context of a low altitude, night-time operational jump. For special operations, the highly reliable Type X was used as early as 1942. Black canopies were supposed to be issued for such operations but several agent accounts confirm the existence of camouflaged, greenish or even white canopies. The reputation of reliability of the Type X was such that the use of a reserve parachute was not deemed necessary until 1952.

The landing position, known as the Parachute Landing Fall (PLF) was devised by RAF Lieutenant John C. Kilkenny and it was also adopted by the US armed forces in 1943. Kilkenny also invented a series of ground exercises and drills meant to prepare the aspiring parachutist for the jump.

Above left.
Type X Parachute with the second type of harness on which the « Quick Release » opening system is permanently held to the harness by a fifth strap.
(Photo et collection E. Lefebvre)

Above right.
Type X Parachute with the first type of harness on which the « Quick Release » opening system marked V 04770 is only held in place by four buckles attached to the straps.
(E. Lefebvre collection)

Left.
Type X Parachute, rear view of a second generation « Quick Release » opening system. An extra piece of metal has been added to permanently link the opening system to the harness.
(E. Lefebvre collection)

Type X Mk I parachute

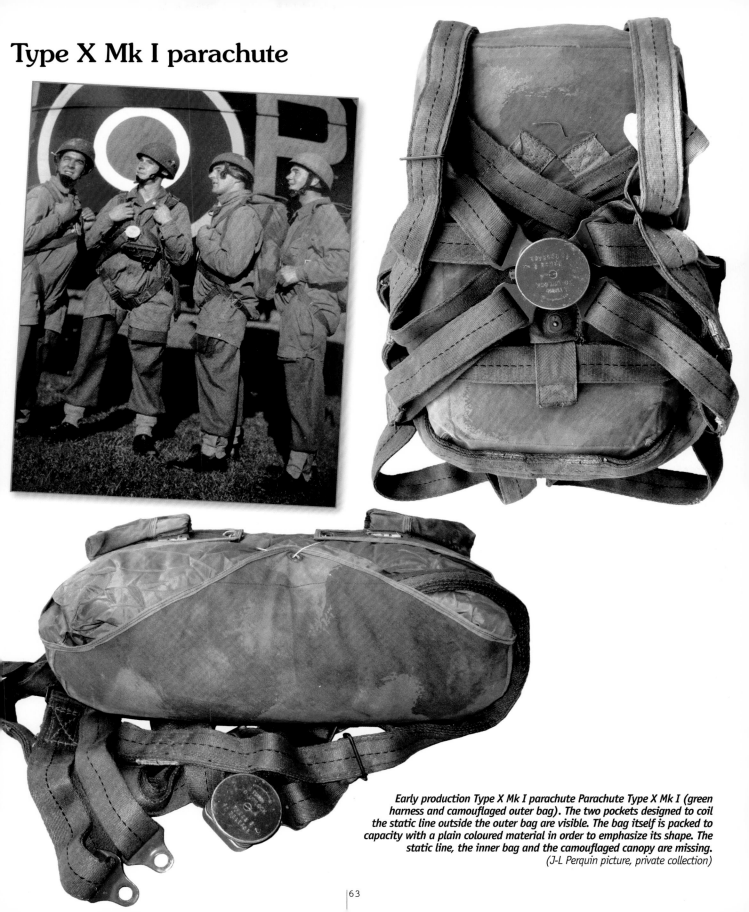

Early production Type X Mk I parachute Parachute Type X Mk I (green harness and camouflaged outer bag). The two pockets designed to coil the static line outside the outer bag are visible. The bag itself is packed to capacity with a plain coloured material in order to emphasize its shape. The static line, the inner bag and the camouflaged canopy are missing.

(J-L Perquin picture, private collection)

Type A parachute

Below.
The camouflaged canopy of Robert Boiteux a.k.a « Nicolas », a British agent belonging to the SOE F Spruce network. He was dropped with Bob Sheppard on 2 June 1942 at 0200 hours near Anse, 25 km North of Lyons. He returned to London thanks to a Hudson Pick-up on 19 August 1943 (Operation « Dyer », 16 km North of Angers). Having the same dimensions as a Type X canopy, its 60 cm apex seems to indicate it is a Small « A » type. A canvas label bears the following mention: GQ 60250.
(Centre d'Histoire de la Résistance et de la Déportation de Lyon).

Next page.
An agent ready to jump from a Withley bomber. He is wearing an early type overall with a collar and a Sorbo helmet. It is also possible to notice the RAF « Observer » type of harness with its straps attached to the outer bag which was itself in turn attached to the inside of the fuselage.
(Drawing by Magali Masselin)

THIS PARACHUTE was developed for special operations when only two or three paras needed to be dropped at a time. Its main peculiarity was that the equipment (suitcase or bergen) was placed on the suspension lines, between the canopy and the parachutist. The design was based on the parachutes used by balloon crewmembers in which the inner bag was fixed to the inside of the dropping plane and the parachutist was only wearing a harness. When used from a fast moving aircraft rather than from a static balloon, this system proved to be quite unreliable and several incidents and injuries resulted from its use.

Two types of canopies could be used: the standard X Type which measured 28 ft. in diameter (8.5 m) and was known as « small A » or the larger, 32 ft. (9.75 m) canopy with a 2 ft. (60 cm) apex known as « large A ».

The canopy was linked to a large bag which included a padded compartment. This compartment was linked to the parachute by a series of D rings, hence the fact it was also sometimes refered to as the « D » Type. Two 12 ft. (3.65 m) straps were hooked to the harness normally issued to observers. Once the canopy had deployed, the agent, dangling from the two straps, would float down to the ground with his equipment placed over his head.

This peculiar system was found to be most useful when fragile equipment had to be delivered because once the agent was on the ground, the canopy would land very gently since it was then only supporting between 40 and 60 lb. (18 to 27 kg).

In his memories published in December 1952 under the title of "Two eggs on my plate" a Norwegian SIS veteran by the name of Oluf Reed Olsen gave some more details on the complex operation of this parachute which he used during the night of the 19th to the 20th of April 1943. The equipment (in that case a bundle) was indeed placed in a rubberized enveloppe located above the parachutist.

Before the agent jumped, this rubberized enveloppe was placed near the jump hole, linked to the harness of the parachutist. When he jumped, the 12 ft. (3.65 m) straps pulled the bundle which then went straight through the hole. The parachute, with a 32 ft. (9.75 m) canopy, was fitted to the top of the bundle.

The top of the parachute was hooked to a 16 ft. (4.87 m) steel cable which itself was linked to a string which had a 225 lbs. (102 kg) breaking point. The steel cable was attached to the plane. The man-bundle assembly first fell for the length of the steel cable which then pulled the parachute for a total length. The steel cable remained attached to the aircraft. The man-bundle assembly fell for the length of the steel cable which in turn led to the opening of the parachute for a total of 30 ft. (9.14 m).

In summary, the complete sequence meant that the parachutist would experience a 62 ft. (19 m) fall before his parachute was completely open: 12 ft. (3.65 m) for the straps, then 3 ft. (91 cm) for the bundle, then 16 ft. (4.87 m) for the steel cable and finally 30 ft. (9.14 m) for the parachute. The equipment bag would add another 89 lbs. (40 kg) comprising two handguns, several civilian suits, two days of rations in a watertight container (RAF rations composed of condensed food, chocolate, raisins etc.) and of course a radio set.

It is noteworthy that with such a parachute, the agent could not pull on his risers to counter-act the speed of the wind or avoid a land obstacle. This still is to this day, standard operating procedure when conducting a static-line night jump but it is worth remembering it.

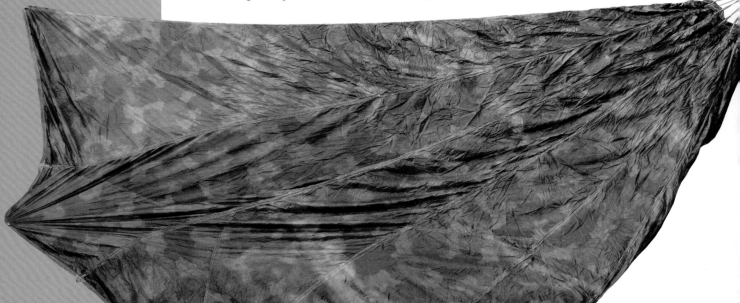

The camouflaged canopy of Bob Sheppard's parachute which remained stuck on the roof of the Gendarmerie in the town of Anse in the Rhône département after his landing there during the night of the 2nd of June 1942.
(Mairie d'Anse)

Ci-contre.
SOE shovel for parachutists (SOE Catalogue reference: G 74). This tool was meant to help rapidly bury all traces of the landing of an agent (Parachute, overall, helmet and special bags). The blade of this spade is heart-shaped with sharpened edges. The top of the blade is upturned to give a foot-hold.
Dimensions:
Blade: Length: 230 mm
Width: 160 mm
Weight: 900gr
Handle: Length: 546 mm
Diameter: 38 mm
Assembled: Length: 730 mm
Width: 160 mm
(J-L Perquin, private collection)

Right.
Rear of the shovel pouch with the handle slid into its sheet.
(J-L Perquin, private collection)

Roach/Mackerel mission parachuting instructions

BCRA memo 644/F.F. dated 23 June 1942 addressed to Capitaine Bienvenue:
1. Roach Major will jump with a large « A » holding his clothes and Roach Alpha's radio set.
2. Roach Minor will jump with a small « A » holding Roach's radio set as well as the reception lamps.
3. Mackerel will jump with a « statichute »
4. In addition, a bundle will hold the following:
- Roach Minor's clothes
- Mackerel's clothes
- Mackerel's radio set (in Mackerel's suitcase)
- Three typewriters (one will be placed in Roach Minor's suitcase)
Total :
- 3 radio sets (small)
- 3 suitcases filled with clothes
- 3 typewriters
- 4 reception lamps complete with spare batteries
The agents will jump in the above-mentioned sequence. The bundle may be dropped first, depending on its weight and on the wind speed on the release point.

This memo confirms the existence of two canopy sizes (Small A et Large A) and it illustrates the fact that three different types of parachutes could be used for the same drop!

This mission was dropped a month latter, on 25 July 1942 by a 138 Squadron Halifax piloted by Flight Lieutenant Wodzicki on DZ « Monge » near Coursages, 10 km South West of Montluçon in the Allier département. The real names of the agents were Jean Ayral (Compagnon de la Libération, MC) a.k.a Pal and his radio operators François Briant a.k.a Pal-W and Daniel Bouyjou-Cordier (Compagnon de la Libération) a.k.a Bip-W.

Roach Major who had jumped with a large « A », landed on his head, his feet caught in the suspension lines, a quite common occurrence with the Type « A »:
- 15 February 1941 Maurice Duclos a.k.a St Jacques brock both legs on landing.
- 7 August 1941 G. Turck belonging to the SOE F / Corsican network got injured on landing.
- 9 December 1941 Edgard Tupet-Thomé from the BCRA landed on his head, his feet caught in the suspension lines and his radio operator Joseph Piet broke a leg.
- 1 May 1942 Lucien Montet from the BCRA got injured on landing.
- 29 May 1942 a BCRA radio operator got killed on landing near Saint Etienne.
- 1 July 1942 Tony Brooks landed horizontaly…
- 26 July 1942 Orabona, a radio operator from the BCRA broke both his legs and crushed his thorax on landing. He died the next day.
- 31 July 1942 Two SOE F agents, Claude de Baissac and Henry Peulevé got injured on landing.
- 17 November 1942 Gustave Bieler from SOE F, injured his spine on landing…

When looking closely at period pictures, one can determine that, in 1942, Robert Sheppard and Tony Brooks jumped with camouflaged-canopy parachutes. Tony Brooks' parachute was an Type « A » which finally was withdrawn from service in 1943. There are no known surviving Type « A » parachutes or even other pictures of it. Lieutenant-colonel Aasland from Norway has drawn our attention to the existence of an incomplete Type « A » harness in the collections of Norwegian museums and it is thanks to this artefact that we were able to identify the parachute visible on the Citerne family pictures.

This harness is also green in colour and it is fitted with D-rings just like those that are visible at chest level on one of René Citerne's pictures.

On 4 June 1942, Pierre Brossolette also used a Type « A » to jump into the Chalon-sur-Saône area. After landing, he told François Chatelin, a member of the reception committee belonging to the Marco Polo network « When the'chute opened, I nearly caught my suitcase on my bloody face! »[1]

Daniel Cordier, Jean Moulin's radio operator and personal assistant whose jump we have mentioned earlier cannot remember having ever jumped with a parachute strapped to his back, either in Tattoon Park or on his infiltration jump. (2009 interview with the author).

Of note, all the early canopie (pre-1942), both for personnel and equipment drops that have survived to this day are of the camouflage type.

1. February 2005 interview with François Chatelin.

Above.
After the liberation of France, René Citerne wears the overall, the Sorbo helmet and the parachute harness of Tony Brooks. His father holds the camouflaged canopy. A close look at the picture reveals that it is an early type of overall (position of the three fasteners and inclusion of a collar). The Sorbo helmet is much lighter in shade than those issued latter in the war that were black. The parachute is an « A » Type which was used by clandestine agents at the beginning of the war. The two hooks that were holding the parachutist's luggage between him and the canopy can easely be seen on the ground.
(Citerne, Bruno Barthelot collection)

The early jump over

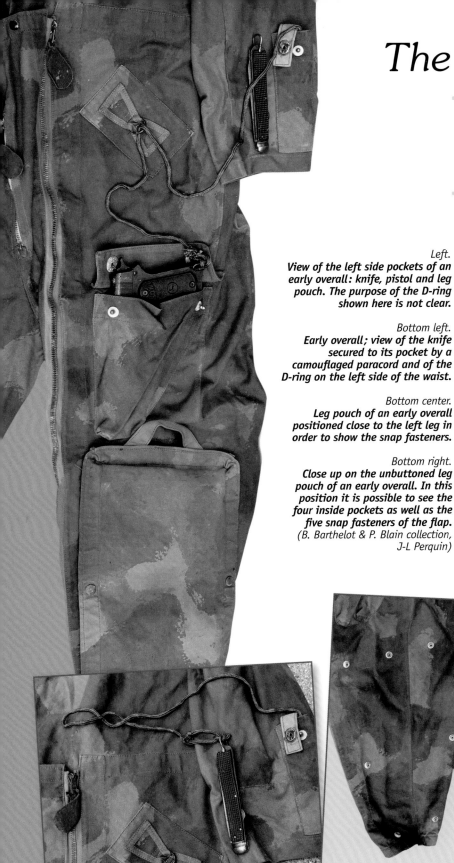

Left.
View of the left side pockets of an early overall: knife, pistol and leg pouch. The purpose of the D-ring shown here is not clear.

Bottom left.
Early overall; view of the knife secured to its pocket by a camouflaged paracord and of the D-ring on the left side of the waist.

Bottom center.
Leg pouch of an early overall positioned close to the left leg in order to show the snap fasteners.

Bottom right.
Close up on the unbuttoned leg pouch of an early overall. In this position it is possible to see the four inside pockets as well as the five snap fasteners of the flap.
(B. Barthelot & P. Blain collection, J-L Perquin)

Researches on SOE overalls have led to the discovery of a specific set of an overall and two pouches cut in the same type of material; they originate from the field and can be dated back to 1942. Currently five such overalls have been located in French collections including one in the museum of the Ecole des Troupes Aéroportées (French Armed Forces Airborne School located in Pau). A Norwegian museum also has one of these overall in its collections. The two pouches were used during the « blind » insertion of British agent Richard « Tony » Brooks a.k.a Alphonse during the night of the 1st to the 2nd of July 1942 in the Château de Bas Soleil, 4 km North of Saint Léonard de Noblat in the Haute-Vienne département. Recovered by the Citerne family, Brooks'parachuting equipment (including a « Sorbo » helmet, an overall, a leg pouch, another camouflaged pack similar to an outer bag, a knife an an « A » Type parachute with a camouflaged canopy) remained hidden for the duration of the war. When liberation came, René Citerne had a picture taken of him with all this equipment. A close examination of those pictures has led to the positive identification of one of the early overall (series of snap fasteners on the bottom of the left leg, location of the three zippers as well as the inclusion of a collar).

The overall was designed to protect the agents from injuries and from getting dirty on landing but thanks to the leg pouches it also allowed them to carry emergency equipment.

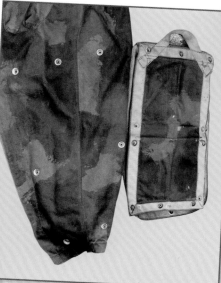

...d its accessories

Similar in design to an RAF flying overall, this early version can be distinguished from latter versions through the following details:
- Collar design
- The zipper is not full length; it stops at chest level. The zipper is located in the middle of the overall and it bears the following markings on its metal tab: « AM » (Air Ministry) and the Royal crown. This part is attached to the rest of the overall by a pair of snap fasteners.
- The lower part has two zippers with the same markings as well as a fly. The strap of the fly is marked « Made in England DOT »
- No inside pocket
- Above the pistol pocket, on the left hip, a reinforced material panel receives a ring probably designed to be used in conjonction with a pistol lanyard.
- Two outside leg pockets (pistol on the left) closing with two american-made « Lift The Dot », snap fasteners.
- Seven snap fasteners on the outside of the bottom left leg in order to attach a pouch carrying emergency equipment such as maps, radio codes, documents, survival rations and first aid kit. These items were moved to inside pockets in the later versions of the overall.
- A survival knife pocket located at the

Early overall with the leg pouch. Notice the switchblade knife secured to the sleeve pocket with camouflaged paracord as well as the 32 ACP Colt pistol.
(B. Barthelot & P. Blain collection, J-L Perquin)

Right left.
Close-up on the right leg pocket « Lift the Dot » snap fasteners on an early overall.

Right center.
AM (Air Ministry) marking and royal crown on the top central zipper of an early overall.

Right.
Made in England DOT marking on the fly zipper of an early overall.
(B. Barthelot & P. Blain collection, J-L Perquin)

69

bottom of the left sleeve. It closes with a strap with an american-made « Lift The Dot », snap fastener. A lanyard (a camouflaged parachute suspension-line) ties the survival knife to the overall.

Another version has also been identified (only one is known to be in existence). It differs from the previous one through the following details:
- The central zipper has a different marking on the its tab, an horizontal « S ».
- The two zippers located on the legs are shortened and located on the bottom of each leg, the two panels being now sewn up to the waist.
- The survival knife pocket is now sewn to the the top of the left shoulder. Nevertheless, it is likely that this pocket has been moved from its original location on the bottom of the left sleeve as there are traces of its previous position there.

It is very likely that this overall was in fact identical to the other four but that it was for some undetermined reasons altered after having been issued.

It seems that the very first helmet used by the SOE was the Sorbo helmet but in a grey colour which was lighter than the black colour used at the end of the war. The Sorbo helmet was the first training helmet used by the trainee parachutists of the British armed forces. Very simple in design, it was made up of slices of Sorbo rubber glued together. It offered a decent, all round level of protection to the head; on the ear flaps, two pieces of strong canvas, either white or green, held two canvas straps used

Above.
Equipment seized on Robert Sheppard after his landing on the roof of the Anse en Beaujolais Gendarmerie on the 2nd of June 1942. A Sorbo helmet and an SOE shovel case are in evidence.
(SHD)

Right.
Robert Bennes'« Sorbo » helmet. He was parachuted from Algiers at 0030 hours on 15 March 1944 on DZ « Ski » in Croix-Régis on the heights over Condrieu near Vienne. He was initialy supposed to be the commander of the Isère département BOA but he had to immediatly replace SAP R1 Venner « Guy » who had been arrested on 13 March. He thus was put in charge of the para drops and radio operators in the Vercors area. His helmet was donated in 1966 to the CHRD by the French Embassy in the Congo Brazzaville.
(J-L Perquin)

Tony Brooks'sleeve knife. It is a foldable switchblade knife with a single blade. It is similar to the two knives seized and pictured by the gendarmes in Robert Sheppard's kit after his landing on the roof of the Anse Gendarmerie in the Beaujolais region on 2 June 1942.
(J-L Perquin)

Left.
SOE overboots made of dark blue canvas. They were tied with laces at three different levels. The first type of overboots had a sole and an heel made of « Sorbo » rubber. Another version was also produced with a leather sole. Designed as a one size fits all, they were big enough to accomodate all shoe sizes. They were meant to complement the overall and to insure that the agents would not soil their shoes on landing and while moving across the fields. The reference in the SOE catalogue was J 223. No markings. Weight of the « Sorbo » rubber version: 1.1 Kg for a pair.
(C. Roussel, privatecollection)

to buckle up the helmet. It remained in service in Ringway until the Bungey helmet, which was both better designed and sturdier, was accepted into service.

All along the war, agents also used it for operational jumps. One such helmet can be identified in the pictures taken by the French Gendarmerie after the arrest of Robert Sheppard after he landed on the Anse Gendarmerie station in the Beaujolais region, 25 km North of Lyons on 2 June 1942 at 02 : 00. A Bungey helmet was also used by Raymond Mocquet a.k.a « Vermuge » belonging to the « DARU » Sussex mission who jumped on 4th August 1944 near Sez…and on April 1945 in Jessore, India, with the DGER Commandos. These helmets are extremly rare because they were produced in small numbers and because rubber deteriorates rapidly.

Above.
Number 2 aid kit and its instructions. Placed in one of the inside pockets of the SOE overall, it was composed of: 10 laxative pills, 8 doses of dehydrated magnesium sulfate, 20 doses of Aspirine, 1 iodine bar, 20 Halozone tabs for water purification, some cotton wool, different types of plasters, safety pins, three vials of morphine, foot powder, a tube of Sulfanilamide gel, some ointment, 12 morphine pills and a thermometer.
(C. Roussel, private collection)

Above and below.
Camouflaged bag used in June 1942 by Tony Brooks. Interestingly, it can be turned inside-out, offering four protective flaps (two with snap fasteners) in order to secure it around the parachutist's body during the jump. At this stage, it has not been possible to determine whether this bag was worn in the front in order to carry some equipment or in the back as a sort of spinal protection (this particular type of overall having no padded back).
(J-L Perquin, B. Barthelot collection)

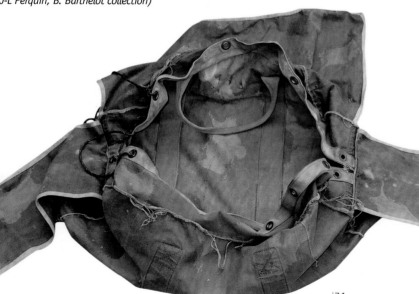

The only visible marking on Tony brooks'bag, near one of the handles: #154.
(J-L Perquin, B. Barthelot collection)

Other types of S[

No LESS than two other variants have been identi-fied, depending on the inclusion of pockets. They were produced either in a sturdy white or camou-flaged material and were available in four sizes.

The overall was fitted with three metal zippers complete with leather tabs. Two large two-way zippers were sewn on the front, allowing for the complete opening of the overall (the central piece remaining attached to the back as with the Deni-

Left.
11th of August1944, RAF Harrington, « Anis » mission. One of the agents gives a kiss to Cécile Pichard before heading for the B-24 from which he will soon jump. Notice he is wearing an overall with the additional small pockets on the back.
(National Archives)

Below.
Inside pockets of the SOE overall: on the left the document pockets, in the middle the opening for the back pocket, on the right, the pocket for the shovel.
(Phillipe Chapilllon, private collection)

Right.
Front view of an SOE overall.
(J-L Perquin, private collection)

Below.
Details of the extra back pocket positioned on the right.
(Laurent Jacquet collection)

Operations Executive (SOE) jumpsuits

son smock), the third zipper and a 20 cm long fly being located in the central part of the garment. Each of the zipper tabs bore a « made in England » marking. The only other marking was the size reference located in the middle of the inside back piece. A leather strap in the back of the collar was designed to attach the helmet. The overall was loose fitting enough to allow the agent to wear two civilian coats underneath it if necessary.

All the pockets closed with snap fasteners.

Outside pockets

A pistol pocket was located on the left thigh; it closed with snap fasteners. At the beginning of the war, the agents used .32 ACP (7.65 mm) pistols, generally a Browning 1910 or a Colt 1903 (the SOE had tasked one of its laboratories to acquire weapons of civilian origin or dating back to WW1 in order to issue its agents with « sterile » weapons). Later during the war, .45 ACP Colt 1911 A1 pistols were also issued.

A pocket for the escape knife was located on the outside of the bottom left sleeve. Closing with snap fasteners, it was within easy reach. A multi-bladed knife tied to a lanyard was used by the agent in order to cut trough risers or suspension lines had he landed in a tree.

The overall were fitted with a large outside pocket sewn to the back panel but which opened from the inside of the gar-

Back cushion placed in the inside overall pocket.
(J-L Perquin)

Above.
Back view of an SOE overall.
(J-L Perquin, private collection)

Above left.
Detail of the markings found on the cushion
(C. Roussel, private collection)

Left.
Back cushion laid next to its pocket.
(J-L Perquin)

73

The SOE jump helmet

Produced in the same strong canvas fabric and same colours (green and brown camouflage or white) as the jump overall it was available in four sizes. Two rims, one crown shaped around the head and another one cresting the top of the helmet offered good shock protection. Flaps covered the ears. The helmet was buckled up through a removable, light leather chin cup which held to the helmet through sheet metal buckles. The central part was made of chamois skin.

An oxygen mask with intercom system could be attached to the front portion of the helmet through four snap fasteners. A light leather strap was sewn to the back of the helmet in order to link it up to the buckled strap found on the collar of the jump overall.

Catalogue references:
22C 965 (size 1)
22C 966 (size 2)
22C 967 (size 3)
22C 968 (size 4)
Weight: 227 grams.

Very light Mica glasses fitted with an elastic band were sewn to the back of the helmet. Those glasses had a fluffy lining.

In side view of the SOE parachuting goggles. Nowadays, they are very difficult to find as they were very fragile…
(J-L Perquin, private collection)

Flask, large type (24 dl) belonging to Raymond Marmande, of the Proust mission « CHAT », parachuted on 30 August 1944 in Osne le Val, Haute Marne département.
(J-L Perquin, private collection)

Below.
Grey survival knife used by Sussex agent Pierre Verges d'Espagne. A marking (RD 354051) is visible on the handle as well as a malta cross and a six-way star.
(Soulier, Musée Sussex)

Left.
SOE shovel Web pouch. The complete set is made up of a green Web pouch fitted with pockets for the blade and the handle of the airborne forces' shovel. This pouch was attached to the Web belt and to the thigh with a leg strap.
(J-L Perquin, private collection)

ment. This pocket was meant to house a cushion which was supposed to pad the back of the agent. It was wide enough to accomodate a small suitcase. On some overall, on the outside of this large pocket, two small additional pockets were located at armpit level. The exact destination of those pockets is not known but they likely were grenade pockets.

The inside of the overall was fitted with several pockets:

On the left thigh, roughly at the same level as the pistol pocket, a pocket was added to house the shovel blade of the special shovel designed to bury the parachuting equipment after the jump; another long and narrow pocket took the shovel handle. Those two pockets were lined with a thick layer of felt in orde to protect the agent on landing.

Inside the right thigh, three pockets also closed with snap fasteners (a large and two small ones) were meant to receive a first aid kit, a dynamo powered torch…)

In the middle of the back, the opening of the back pocket.

In order to illustrate the use of those pieces of equipment, here is an extract from the memories of Paul Carron de la Carrière, a member of the « Gilbert » Jedburgh team who jumped on 10 July 1944 on DZ « Guide » in Scaer near Coadry in the Finistère département.

In another pocket was positioned the escape and evasion kit, complete with files, hooks, nylon thread, small hand razor and shaving cream because as our British instructors used to say « an unkeept man is quickly spotted », pills against drowziness, a vial of morphine and its syringe and probably some cyanide pills in case one had to commit suicide.

That was some serious stuff!

My team and I had prefered the canvas, training type helmet and I reckon that our three helmets made three Breton maquisards happy.

For my part, I had planned an ever more sought after « goody ». In order to cushion our landing, we had a Dunlopillo pillow affixed to our lower back. I had estimated that once I had done my PLF on French soil, it would become all but useless. I had thus prepared a pillow made of….tobacco. It was an army green towel that a service tailor had sown in a triangular shape after having it stuffed full of pipe tobacco (NAAFI tobacco was cheap). This new type of nappy was thus fixed between my legs, each corner held by a safety pin. I can't recall when we distributed the tobacco but I still can picture the maquisards lining up in a queue to receive their small share of delicious blond tobacco. Not only was I happy to give those men

such pleasure but I also reveled in the knowledge that I had outfoxed the Customs officers, not that we saw a lot of those honourable civil servants when we crossed the border in a, it's fair to say, rather unconventional way.

Abstract from *Le chapeau de Napoléon est-il toujours à Perros Guirec?*
By Paul Carron de la Carrière

Above.
One of a series of different added protection that could be sown inside an SOE overall. This 2.5 cm thick sheet of « Sorbo »rubber wrapped in canvas was supposed to offer some added protection on landing. This particular item comes from the « Dentelle » Sussex mission which was parachuted in Alençon on 7 July 1944.
(Soulier, Musée Sussex)

The Bungey training helmet

Introduced in 1942 and used for the rest of the the war, the Bungey was a rubber training helmet. It was a light design made of beige canvas material covering a crown made of foam and rubber.

Inside the inside top lining, adjustment to the required size was achieved through an hemline with a leather lace. Canvas material flaps covered the neck and ears and doubled as straps to buckle the helmet up. Bungey helmets never had metallic buckles. Three main types of helmets existed, the difference being in the flaps. They were either plain, with two gromlets positioned at ear level (in metal or brass and of varying diameters depending on the manufacturers) or with holes but no metal gromlets. Sizes 1 and 2 are known to exist. Different qualities of canvas material were used, depending on the manufacturer and on the availability of materials when the orders were placed. A white label was sewn to the inside of the helmet (top rear). Those helmets can sometimes be offered for sale to collectors but copies abound.

When the helmet was worn for parachute operations, the straps were knotted under the chin and then rolled and tucked so they would not come undone under the effect of the wind when exiting an airplane or a balloon.

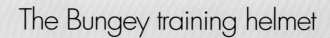

(J-L Perquin)

Civilian clothing

THE DRAWING OF CLOTHING and equipments by the agent marked the last stage of his training before leaving on mission. This was the final touch that would help him to be invisible to the enemy and to blend in with the local population.

Therefore, a large variety of clothes had to be managed in vast quantity in order to provide the full range of men's clothing and personal equipment. In addition, it had to be available in all sizes. To give an idea of the amount of pieces of equipment and clothing drafted by the agents, 8,665 items were distributed during a single month, in 1944; the stock then consisted of 20,040 different items.

Regarding women's clothing, it seemed more convenient to interview directly the agents by selecting the dress styles, etc.., via foreign periodicals and newspapers in order to get the appropriate articles for the country of destination. This method required individual "shopping trips" for each female agent and the results gave them full satisfaction.

As for men's clothing, it was more difficult to get the appropriate clothes even though it was absolutely necessary as British clothes would not pass the test of the most perfunctory control in an occupied country. Thus, SOE made contacts with firms that were importing continental clothing or manufacturing goods that were sold on the continent and that would have mainland tailors in their staff.

One of the solutions was to make good copies by paying particular attention to details, woven materials, colors, buttons, cottons, finish, cuts, trims and other details that would draw the attention of a professional. The clothes had to be almost indistinguishable from a continental production. They were made without any manufacturers or retailers marks or indications of sizes because that would have helped the enemy to identify the supposed supplier, who could in turn deny having supplied the garment thus unknowingly betraying the agent. There were exceptions to this rule when the cover of the agent needed to be linked to a particular city, region or a manufacturer, then brands were copied and sewn on. This process required to weave copies of manufactures'labels. A significant amount of authentic continental clothing were obtained from refugees.

The « Aubrey » Jedburgh team is one of the few teams to have jumped operationaly dressed in civilian attire because its area of operation was located in the North-East of Paris. The quality and fine cut of the suits provided by the SOE stores is much in evidence here. Left to right : Free French Lieutenant A. Chaigneau a.k.a « Koldare » a.k.a J. Telmon killed on the 27th August 1944 near Oissery in the Seine-et-Marne département; center British Captain Godfrey Marchant a.k.a « Rutland », team leader; seated, the British radio operator, an NCO by the name of Ivor Alfred Hooker a.k.a « Thaler ». They were parahuted from « Fightin' Sam », a B-24 (serial number D-42-40506-R) piloted by an American officer named Moser on 12 August 1944 at 01 : 55 hours at Plessis-Belleville during Operation Spiritualist 6. (National Archives)

Most of the clothes were new when they left the stores, but they were artificially "aged" to give an appearance of used and worn clothing before being provided to the officers and this, always in conjunction with his cover story. The state of wear was perfectly rendered by appropriate specialists.

The final touch of the equipment was given by the supply of watches, cigarette holders, wallets, pocket knives, ink pens, belts, wallets, lighters and suitable handbags. All these items were issued after a careful study of the way of life in occupied territories; Most of these items came directly from refugees or from pre-war importers, some were obtained by other government services.

Finally, brushes and leather products were used to hide codes, money, documents, etc. (hair and shaving brushes, clothes and tooth brushes, shoe brush, purse, briefcases, etc.).

Above and left.
On those two pictures taken on Harrington Airfield on 11 August 1944, it is possible to identify Cécile Pichard from the « Anis » mission. On the left, a British officer and a Staff Sergeant help an agent to don his jump overall over his coat. On the top picture, it is also possible to make out some of the agent's civilian clothing.
(National Archives)

Equipment given to an agent leaving on a mission.

Memo n° 374 from the BCRA (OP bloc, MP/PA, 4°Bureau) dated 10 of March, 1944 listed the typical equipment given to an agent leaving on a mission.

An automatic pistol with 50 rounds, a switchblade folding knife, a commando dagger, a compass, a field dressing, an electric flashlight with a spare battery, a flask of rum, an army type emergency ration, a battle dress, a pair of gloves, a rubber helmet, a lower back protector, a pair of boot protector, a 2 day ration, a woolen Balaklava, 2 pair of shoes, 2 suits, an overcoat, a trench coat, 6 pairs of socks, a pair of slippers, 4 boxer shorts, 4 vests, 6 shirts, 2 ties, 4 woolen vests, a pair of gloves, 2 pyjamas, a toiletry bag, a sweater, a suitcase, 2 napkins, 6 handkerchieves, a dressing gown, 1 pullover.

If the agent was parachuted, two pairs of RAF gloves (one silk and one leather) were added as well as a jumpsuit and ankle bandages. Ten days before leaving, the suitcase and its content were controlled at N°1 Dorset Square. French coins and cinema tickets were added.

The day before departure, the agent was issued British ration cards for a week… this enabled him to have a big breakfast on the day of the operation (eggs, bacon, pork chops, sausages, butter, jam, bread and coffee); this was an incredible luxury in England during the war and it did surprise the agents who were just about to depart!

An underground shooting range was located in a nearby subway, allowing the agent to test fire their weapons before deporting on their missions.

PARACHUTE OPERATIONS

It was during the full moon of the 13th of June 1941 that Philippe Vomecourt (SOE) received the first supply drop of arms and ammunition in support of an operational agent. This operation was performed on his property of « Bas-Soleil », twenty kilometers from Limoges. This was the first supply drop of weapons as well as the first landing strip marking on the same area near Saint Leonard de Noblat. The larger number of aircraft assigned to special squadrons and landing strips led to the increasing of the number a large increase in the number of containers and packages dropped in support of Résistance movements.

The specific organization of French networks

Above.
Container drop by Halifax.
(Aldo Boccone collection)

Right.
Non regulation BOA Bloc Nord badge. A parachute bears a shield with a Cross of Lorraine. The suspension lines are superimposed with Armée de l'Air (French Air Force) wings.
(S. Larcher Collection, J-L Perquin)

Next page, top left.
A non-regulation BOA badge incorporating a parachute as well as a propeller, probably as a reminder of the BOA role in pick-up operations.
(E. Micheletti collection)

THE LIAISON OFFICERS of the French BCRA (SOE RF) received their first parachute drops from early 1942. In November 1942, given the size of the organization and the growth of air activities, Jean Moulin decided to create a specialized department, stationed in the yet unoccupied South zone of France, called the SOAM (Service d'Opérations Aériennes et Maritimes–Department of Maritime and Air Operations). Soon after, still in 1942, he stood up a similar organization in North and West area (those were occupied areas), that took the name of BOA (Bureau of Air Operations).

In April 1943, after a serie of arrests, the Southern department was reorganized and became the COPA (Centre d'Opérations de Parachutages et d'Atterrissage–Parachutings and Landing Operations Center). The COPA lost most of its leadership on 21 June 1943 when Klaus Barbie, the regional head of the Gestapo, arrested the main Resistance leaders at a meeting in Caluire in the Lyons suburbs. Paul Rivière was urgently recalled from London to take over the control of the network, which changed its name again for security reasons to SAP (Service des Atterrissages et Parachutages–Parachutings and Landings Service). The importance of the air links grew rapidly and from the Spring of 1943, the BOA was able to provide the BCRA with almost 500 dropping zones and it was able to carry out 100 to 200 operations a month. According to the officials in charge of the disbandment of the BOA, its losses totaled 900 deads, of 200 of which having been shot or killed in action. The number of deportees that were eventually repatriated was estimated at 800… this is a rough estimate as the disappearance of many BOA officers meant the exact organization was never fully known when Liberation came. 2,000 dropping zones were approved by the RAF which means that 15,000 team members were involved. The number of officialy sanctioned resistance fighters approved by the officials in charge of the disbandment of the BOA is much lower.

Above.

Michel Pichard a.k.a: Pic–Bel–Gaus pictured in August 1944 in the Haute-Marne département. He is wearing a British uniform with the « light bulb » parachute badge on the bottom of the left sleeve. Having joined the Free French forces in August 1941, he spent a month in Camberley where he was promoted to the rank of aspirant (candidate officer) before being posted to the Bureau Central de Renseignements et d'Action (BCRA), the Free French secret services. He did his special training in September 1941 and was then infiltrated into the South of Brittany in January 1943. In May 1943, he was posted from the intelligence gathering section to the action section, namely to the Bureau des Opérations Aériennes (BOA, the Air Operations Bureau). In July 1943, he became the national commander of the BOA. Having returned to London in June 1944, he returned to Brittany in July 1944 in order to support the para drop of the Free French SAS of the 2e Régiment de Chasseurs Parachutistes (2°RCP). After this mission and a return to the UK, he was once again parachuted into France during the night of the 11th to the 12th of August 1944 in the Haute-Marne département as the Délégué Militaire Départemental (Departmental Military Delegate). There, he organized several para drops with the departmental FFI Résistance group commander leading to the organization of a 5,000 man strong resistance force. He was made a Compagnon de la Libération by a 16 June 1944 decree. (Josiane Somers collection)

At the beginning, an average operation meant receiving a single plane carrying eight containers and 2 or 3 packages, then the average was 15 containers and 6 packages with the Halifax and then 18 or even 24 containers with the Stirling. Similarly, the number of aircrafts guided towards the same landing strip rose to 3 and often 6.

The maquis areas, in remote and rural regions, allowed operations beyond 15 to 18 containers and 6 packages. Alternate strips were organized in order to allow aircrafts that had not found their DZs, or had found them but thought they were unsatisfactory (no lights) to drop their loads. Standing on high alert during the moon phases, a Eureka beacon and generally a S-Phone, were activated on the drop zones and a large-scale reception committee was waiting to transport these unexpected supplies to nearby caches.

Left.

This badge was issued to parachute-qualified personnel who were not on the posted strength of an airborne unit. Instruction ACI 1274 dated 17 June 1942 authorized a badge depicting a white embroidered parachute on a square-shaped piece of army green material for those personnel who had trained as parachutists but were not, or had never been, posted to an airborne unit. This badge (which was nicknamed the light bulb) was initially sewn at the same place as the para wings. From October 1942, it was moved to the right forearm, 6 inches (15 cm) from the bottom of the battledress or service dress of the officiers. Warrant Officers wore this badge just over their rank badge. Normal issue was two badges per person. This badge was not worn on the overcoat or on the denim battle dress and it was used by the agents of the SOE, the OSS and the BCRA. (E. Micheletti collection)

Above.
RAF Tempsford, the last remaining Gibraltar Farm building pictured in 2009.

Below.
Located close to Tempsford (Bedfordshire), Hasell's Hall housed agents just before they were parachuted into occupied territory or when they had to return to the UK because their missions had to be aborted (picture taken in 2009).
(J-L Perquin)

Below.
Container drop by a Halifax
(Now it can be told, 1946)

	PICK-UP		DROPS	NAVAL OP		TOTAL PER YEAR	
	IN	OUT		IN	OUT	IN	OUT
1940	-	1	3	-	-	3	1
1941	1	5	65	-	-	66	5
1942	25	32	102	-	-	127	32
1943	157	298	198	-	-	355	298
1944	73	95	1 382	-	-	1 455	95
TOTAUX	256	431	1 750	1 500	3 000	3 506	3 431

Left.
**Polish parachutists getting ready
to land with a camouflaged
Type X parachute..**
(Aimé Flaba collection)

Recollections of an agent parachuted into France

An ANONYMOUS AGENT RELATED his recollections of a night jump in the N° 28 issue of « Béret Rouge » magazine:

Tonight was the night. Charles, my team partner and I had lunch at the Brasserie Universelle in Piccadilly once again. Since we have been told this morning that we were going to France, another person has settled inside me, which means that basically there were three of us. This person, invisible to others (at least I hoped), was made of a curious substance, a kind of chemical assembly that had made my throat smaller than usual, which I realized when I tried swallowing the fish-and-chips with little sips of lagger. "Beer is best"…

When arriving at our 2:00 pm appointment, we found the unescapable Security Officer of Her Majesty. Jovial, talkative, we left together towards an airfield in the suburbs, "our" airfield.

Three hours later, the preparations began. An thorough search of our pockets led to the destruction of the last cinema ticket, the discovery of the "Day Ticket", the famous ticket reserved to the "Forces" which allowed, against a small fee, members of the armed forces to travel on all the London public transportation (excluding taxis…) for a day. Needless to say, we French had decided that this ticket would be purchased once and for all. Presented to different controllers, it was never examined closely: this would not have been correct. Only its loss would have deprived us from it. Our money, or what was left of it, was locked away with our British identity cards in an envelope that would only be opened when the Red Cross returned, the papers destroyed.

Dinner. Little is said but we laughed a lot… the story of the aircraft completely empty. Money would be used to play smart Alec. 9:00 pm: we don the equipment. Jumpsuit, with multiple pockets and all of them full of all types of objects: flashlight, emergency ration box, individual bandage, compass, knife, pistol, and so on. To me who had been accustomed to the French Quartermaster of 1940, what a difference! Had we been dealing with them again, we would have been given a sheet of paper full of rubber stamps with the sacred words: « Did not draw anything at the beginning… Will be reminded on arrival ». Oilskin boots, rubber helmet and parachute, we get the lot. A small flask of rum is there too. This is exactly what we had ordered some months earlier.

Previous page.
An original artwork by Joachim Pol based on the author's guidance : under a full moon, a 138 Squadron (NF) Halifax drops an agent into occupied France.

Right.
Stein W. Aasland dressed in full mission suit while carrying out researches on clandestine operations in 1992. The Type X parachute, the overall, the helmet and the overboots are all SOE equipment. The use of RAF flying glove was frequent and they were standard SOE issue.
(Norwegian resistance Museum)

10 : 00 pm. Three Halifax stand in front of us, their black paint giving them a sinister appearance. Handshakes. A WAAF (Women's Auxiliary Air Force) gives us a fraternal kiss and we get on board. "When on board, please sit, put the thermos bottle, the packets of sandwiches and the packet of bandages that you were given close at hand and do not move anymore…" We obey. The engines scream… We take off. We are in August and the sun sets behind the horizon. The nose pressed against the small window of the plane, we can see the countryside rushing below us. One airfield after another. The coast, a fringe of foam indicates the sea. "Sorry Sir." The dispatcher pulls the black-out curtain : it's dark outside now. A blue light glows faintly inside the plane silhouetting us, giving the whole scene a gloomy atmosphere.

The door separating us from the cockpit opens and a giant appears and shout something at us. "France," he yells, pointing to the floor. From our side, the light have been switched off and the window curtain is still drawn. I look and do not see anything at all. "They are going to try the guns," Charles shouts to me, he received that information from the dispatcher, so we do not worry. Explosions followed, short bursts. The aircraft is shaken. I check my watch: almost midnight. It is very cold. I drank some hot tea, spilling half of it on me. Now, I have to get rid of this overflow and let nature follow its course. I walked towards the back of the plane to the latrines, and spends almost twenty minutes there trying to extricate myself from the zipper, trousers buttons and harness strap. On top of that, at the last moment, I was handed a large packet "to give to the receiving Committee as soon as I landed." This package is stuck in my upper chest, like a ventral chute set too high. It bothers me. And it is not the only one that bothers me: the parachute bothers me, as the equipments, even the aircraft bothers me. What the hell am I doing there?

And I resume my thoughts when I return to my seat without having been able to fulfill the mission I had given myself. We must be high, my ears are buzzing. The thoughts of enemy night fighters kept me busy for a moment… I am now busy with the Flak. Instinctively, I move a little on the bench to avoid an imaginary shell that would drill my padded arse.

I slept a little. It is now 1 : 00 am. Within another hour, it will be time. My nose is running and my handkerchief is in my pants'pocket, which is part of my jump suit, which is blocked by the harness. I wipe my nose on my sleeve, ending this delicate operation on the handle of the dagger which is located there. Now I have grazed my nose. How clever of me !

Above.
Norwegian parachutist with a deployed Type X.
(Norwegian Armed Forces Museum, Oslo)

Previous page.
Dorset Square in Marylebone, London. This is where BCRA agents linked up with the SOE RF section in order to draw their last pieces of equipment before departing on their operational missions. A firing range had been arranged in a nearby Tube station to test fire the agents' weapons…
(Josiane Somers collection)

Above.
138 Squadron Halifax dropping parachutists.
(Now it can be told, 1946)

Next page.
Agents under a parachute.
(Norwegian Armed Forces Museum, Oslo)

The light has become stronger. The dispatcher is working on the hatch. It is 1:40 am. He gestures towards us in a friendly way: thumbs up.

Everything goes well. Obviously, viewed from the aircraft, everything looks fine, but if I was asked my opinion, I would say that... yes, everything goes well, obviously. I smile to the dispatcher, a bit like the patient would smile at his dentist before sitting on the chair. He arranges a whole mishmash of straps that are intended to receive our static lines. Now, this is it. It had to happen: the hatch is open. The light is off. The plane circles. The dispatcher speaks in his throat microphone. He looks at us; thumbs-up: eve-rything is more than perfect. It is amazing how well this business is going. Let's hope it lasts... We are told by hand signs to come closer. From both sides of the hatch, the dispatcher hooked our static lines and then showed us the pin so we do not need to worry about that anymore. For my part, my worries are not of this kind, but I worry about the black hole where we'll have to jump in in a moment. To the ear of Charles, who may understand English better than I, the dispatcher speaks with satisfaction. A little devil whispers in my ear that we may return to London. I reject this idea. "He said he saw the lights marking the DZ. Everything is OK..."

Now, inside the plane, we seemed to have gotten into a trance. The dispatcher who no longer was smiling shouts « get ready ». My feet are in the hatch. I am sitting on the edge of my buttocks, the airflow around me, my eyes are on the dispatcher who has raised an arm. Time seems to be standing still. I'm Number One. I'm out. The "Go", my hands in front of my face and then brought back along the body in the attention position, fast flowing air all around me, all that has been mixed into one second. I am descending, it is pitch dark. I take the landing position as I had learnt. I see nothing, absolutely nothing. The air is nice and cool."

Next page top.
Norwegian agent Lars J. Larsen after his landing during Op «Makir» on May 6, 1944 in Eikerwoods, Norway. The SOE overall, Sorbo helmet and Type X parachute with green canopy are evidence.
(Oluf Reed Olsen collection)

Next page bottom.
Early overall and « A » Type parachute: side shot on which it is possible to make out the series of snap fasteners on the bottom of the left leg and the popped collar of the overall. It is fairly obvious that young René Citerne has been unable to don the harness correctly.
(Citerne, Barthelot collection)

Left.
Model wearing a jump suit. Next to him, a container with a black canopy.
(C. Roussel, private collection)

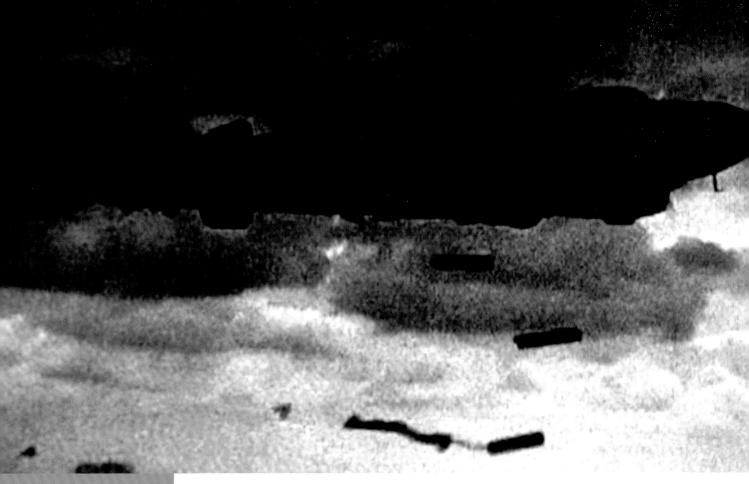

Chronology of a weapon drop

Via his radio operator, the head of the network asks for an equipment drop in a field in an occupied zone. The message gives a list of the required equipment, the grid coordinates of the DZ as well as the personal message for the BBC.

London quickly sends a reply confirming the instructions and announces that the operation is scheduled for the next moon, for example between the 20th to the 26th of this month and between 11:00 pm and 1:00 am GMT, which means between 1:00 am to 3:00 am local time. In summer, the limits are quite close to each others, as the nights are shorter.

The head of the network and his local contact go back to see the farmer responsible for the team tasked with the collection of the equipment after the drop. Everyone knows the principle of personal messages from the BBC.

During the BBC French language broadcast at 7:30 pm, the message is aired once. The French announcer's voice of the English radio is nearly drowned by the strong interferences. The broadcast is finally over…

"And here are some personal messages… ". The first message is not the right one, neither is the second or the third. Then: "Our country is so beautiful, I say, our country is so beautiful." There it is. The men straighten up, the eyes are brighter. For them, this is a first demonstration of power. The text was written here, unbeknownst to all but a few, and now it has just been recited to millions of listeners, while still maintaining secrecy.

This is the beginning of the process.

The farmer and his companions, who live a few minutes away from the DZ were able to listen at home not only the 7:30 broadcast, but also to the 9:15 pm. Thus, they can confirm that the message has really been repeated a second time. The rendez-vous is scheduled for 10:00 pm, at the time of the curfew.

By a full moon, the silhouette of the aircraft with all its lights off will not be visible at more than a mile, whereas the drone of its engines cannot be heard for more than five to six miles at the most.

While waiting, the leader conducts a quick refresher. Three men should be positioned at the vertical of an equilateral triangle oriented so that one corner point to the wind. All three will light a white torch and the man in the wind will light, in addition to his white torch, a red one. The aircraft must release the load directly over the red and white lights so that the wind drift will push the parachutes toward the base of the triangle.

In the meantime, the leader of the reception committee gives some technical information: the aircraft will fly at an altitude of one hundred fifty meters and at a low speed of two hundred miles per hour. It is important that everyone counts the number of parachutes that have opened: this is very important. The wind can Pick-up and scatter them and if the exact number is not known, one can forget one or two on site, which can have very serious consequences.

The moon rises and floods the clearing with silvery light. Not a cloud in sight. H hour has arrived…
— Hush! Silence! Listen, listen!
Yes, a distant sound is heard, and a far-off a series of low stifled grunts "gr… gr… gr… gr…". They become louder, like the pulsations of a soft purr.
— Each man to his position! Turn your lights on as soon as you see mine!
— The men rush to the tips of the triangle.

The growl of the engines becomes louder. The on-site commander lights his torch up and directs it towards the sound. The other lights are switched on. The muffled sound becomes a roar in which one can hear the shrill whistle of the reduction gears. All the men peel their eyes, the plane cannot be far. There. This small black spot which moves quickly in the dark blue sky. The roar swells crescendo. The black spot comes closer and becomes a big plane, which flies at a low altitude, majestically, a little beside the lights, in the thunder of its four engines. A square, twin tail: this is a Halifax. The aircraft disappears into the night and now only a gentle hum can be heard.

The plane has done a dry run on the DZ. Now, it does a wide turn and returns. One must continue to direct the lights towards the sound, and start counting the parachutes…

The roar again. Here it is. This time, it comes right over the DZ.

The noise seems to echo in the sky, the aircraft flies just overhead, its fuselage seems to burst into a bouquet of several round black flowers that it has left in its wake.

One, two, three… five… eight parachutes float down to the ground. Then the tubular containers touch the ground with a clanking noise.

The canopies of the dark parachutes gently land and spread like burst balloons.

Then, it is the scramble to the containers.

Here again the noise of the aircraft, it looks like it is coming back. Perhaps, it has something left to drop.

Indeed, here is the silhouette of the huge black bird. This time, it does not fly towards the lights, but it does a wide circle around the field. The crew tries to make out the reception committee in the darkness to check the accuracy of the drop.

The bomber flies away and disappears into the night. Its hum becomes a whisper and finally vanishes.

The drop went well. The cluster of parachutes landed less than one hundred meters from the lights. One start counting the containers and only find six. Where are the other two? In the darkness, a man comes running.

Above.
Container drop by a Halifax.
(Aldo Boccone collection)

He announces that he found two other parachutes hanging on the trees at the edge of the clearing. That's a total of eight. Indeed, two square packages wrapped in canvas are hanging from the branches.

The containers were carried in the bomb bay of the aircraft – their size and bulk was the same as the 500 lbs. bombs–and they were dropped in clusters, while the packets, as they were lighter, were thrown through the « Joe hole » in the fuselage. That's why they fell a little further. The container was provided with hinges along its entire length and opened into two parts after opening three latches. Within the container, three short and stumpy cylindrical boxes held the equipment. They were heavy and the lids were fitted with wire handles. The canopy and suspension lines of the parachute also had to be recovered and placed in the empty containers. The team removes the boxes from all the containers and begin to carry them through the woods to the opposite edge near the limit of the fields. After a number of return trips, the boxes, the empty containers and the two packages are gathered at the edge of the wood.

Both packages are padded with foam rubber plates; this generally means that they hold sensitive equipment: a new transmitter in the first package and some special items in the second. The containers boxes carry normal supplies such as explosives, weapons and ammunition.

One now has to carry the equipment to the farm.

Among the weapons are a few "goodies" and small gifts: cigarettes, tobacco, chocolate, butter jars, cans of cooking oil, tinned food. The distribution is carried out quickly and it helps establish a human connection with this mysterious HQ located in London.

A patrol leaves to ensure that there is no trace of the operation left in the clearing. The Germans are not kidding with this and the officer in charge of the area has given the following note the widest distribution:

"Anyone who has discovered aircrafts, aircraft parts, materials coming from aircrafts or some object thrown by aviators, is obliged to leave them behind without touching them and, immediately, make a declaration of his discovery to the nearest German authorities, police stations or town halls. The offenders will be liable to hard labor or more severe penalties if necessary."

The operation was a success.

Previous page.
Container drop by a Halifax.
(Josiane Somers collection)

Right.
Agent parachuted with his containers by a Halifax.
(J-L Perquin collection)

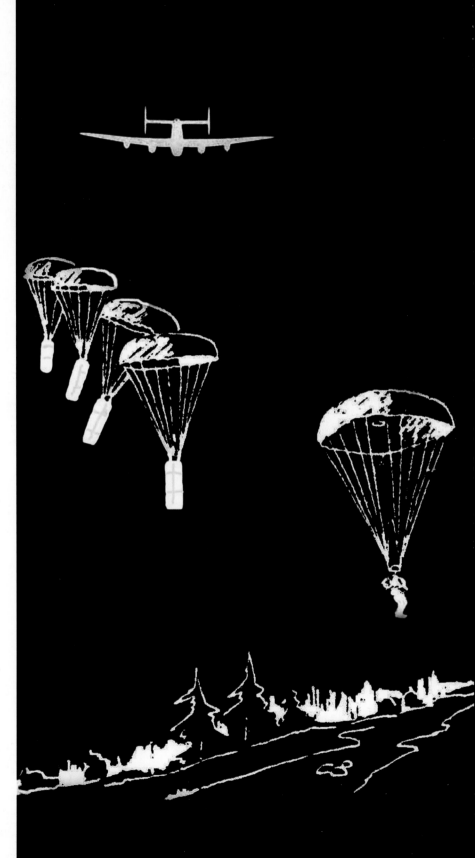

A Pick-up by Lysander

During Operation "Renoir", performed on the night of the 17th to the 18th of July 1943, at Nantheuil-le-Haudoin near Bouillancy in the northeast of Paris, Marie-Madeleine Fourcade, head of the Alliance network, accurately describes her exfiltration:

Marie-Madeleine Fourcade leaves Paris from the Gare de l'Est train station around 5 : 00 pm to link up with "Dallas", her network's BOA team leader. He is accompanied by an aide and two other "out" passengers : Lt. Poulard and a British officer, Michel Gaveau.

They leave the train at Nanteuil-le-Haudouin. At night, they get on a car

Above.
November 1944, Lysander Mk III SD R 9125 piloted by Turner captured in flight. This plane is currently on show at the RAF museum in Hendon and is the last remaining 161 Squadron airplane. Unfortunately, it is missing its external long-range tank. The ladder has been repainted in the Army camouflage pattern. On the other hand, the rear cockpit is still in the SD version.
(Now it can be told, 1946)

and take short cuts before entering a harvested cornfield. The marking team is already there waiting for them.

« Once again, the silhouettes of the team were moving noiselessly in the field. I looked at my watch, it was 0h59 GMT. A few seconds later, a buzzing noise was heard in the distance. A car on the road? The trained ear of Dallas got it right. He switched his flashlight on shining in the direction of the noise and his two assistants did the same. The noise had become that of a powerful motorcycle that would have caught a cold. Soon, we were able to see, to the North West, a form which was coming closer to us. At that time, Cornac began sending its signals "M". "M". "M". "M". Soon, the Lysander replied "R". "R". "R". "R". "R", flashing its position lights.

The flashes stopped and the docile Lysander landed. The plane did a U-turn.

The rear cockpit suddenly opened and three men popped out and drew their luggages with them. They grabbed ours according to the usual ritual and stacked them up in the appropriate hold of the aircraft. They were Georges Lamarque, back from his training course, and our beloved radio operators Rossignol and Stork arriving from Algiers to resume the fight.

I climbed into the cockpit where Poulard and Gaveau had gotten as well. Dallas, clinging at the front, was sharing a few joyful words and little gifts with the RAF pilot,

a friend he had made in London. The hatch was closed and the aircraft began to roll.

We were in the air when I realized that less than seven minutes had elapsed between the beginning and the end of this magic: landing and taking off thirty miles away from Paris, in times of occupation.

The magic went on. The instrument panel now lit the Lysander cabin.

"If you see an enemy plane, press this button to warn the pilot."

"Bon voyage!"

"You will find hot coffee in the flask placed right at your feet, whiskey in the bottle placed left."

As I had been told so often, sitting facing the rear, we were separated from the pilot by the compact mass of the extra fuel tank. He, however, could only see to his front. The only service we could possibly do for this «pigeon» was to report the bird of prey diving into his back. After having poured ourselves a good coffee laced with whiskey, we began to carefully search the sky. The moon was with us in our race to the Channel, and, at medium altitude, the view of France fleeing under us was crushing me. All life seemed to have withdrawn from the body of my country. We flew over the dead cities without smoke, without lights. This was the picture of my despair.

Lieutenant Poulard had not flown since 1940 and his enthusiasm won me over:

— How formidable are these guys, nothing but a compass, nothing but a wild-arse guess ! Look, boss, here is the coast. Hey! Hey! These lights, looks like we are in for a bit of flak ! Wham ! Nice turn on the wing, another miss. Bravo, my friend, I would not have done better!

The sea now was guiding our journey with millions of sparkling wavelets.

A conversation could be heard over the intercom. The pilot had contacted his base. We saw the cliffs of «stronghold» England, then fields, roads, villages and, suddenly, a great whirl of lights, beacons everywhere, a festival of lights. The pilot choose his runway, flared and landed, stopping right in front of a group of officers in green and blue uniforms who greeted us solemnly. The position lights were switched off, leaving us all in a complete blackout.

— Have you had a good trip? Good weather, is it not? Come have something.

RAF personel took charge of the Lysander and suitcases.

— Be careful with the mail, I stupidly said.

— Do not worry about anything yet!

Richards led me to the mess from which we could hear some joyful banter ringing through the black out curtains. Hives also existed here.

When we entered, no one stopped talking, playing or drinking. The arrival, at two o'clock in the morning, of three «pilgrims», unwashed, unkempt, rumpled as rags, did not make any of those young pilots budge ; their composure, boldness and perseverance changed the face of war

Above.
Lysander DG 453 E in flight.

Below.
Lucien Poulard in 1942.
(Josiane Somers collection)

Above.
This Lysander crashed on 31st August 1942 during Operation Boreas II on the «Faisan» strip 1.8 km Nord of Arbigny in the vicinity of Pont de Vaux. Because of faulty landing indications, the plane broke its landing gear and its propeller. Pierre Delaye, the passenger, and W. G. Lockhart the pilot were unscathed. The plane was torched. The pilot returned to London on 13 September 1942.
(Jean-Michel Rémy collection)

Below.
Drawing of a Lysander D from 161 Squadron (MA) .
(J-L Perquin collection)

every minute. In England, one does not ask questions, one just resolves them.

In the cordially smoky atmosphere, with hints of blond tobacco, we were poured all kinds of drinks, we were presented one hundred brands of cigarettes. My reward was to see Poulard, slumped in a comfy chair, his mouth full of a white bread York ham sandwich looking affectionately at his brothers in arms: the officers of the Royal Air Force.

I was expecting being caught in a military maze of barracks and ranking officers, but the cottage which appeared in front of me, hidden in a garden of greenery and flowers, was like those of the nursery rhymes of my childhood. Nothing was missing, the deep comfortably worn sofa, the multicolored binders lining the shelves, the dining table covered with porcelain cups, the China so cherished by the English, and fruit dishes crumbling

with slices of cake, toasts, buns. Under a cozy, a tea pot was smoking and, in front of each guest, scrambled eggs were continuing to cook on their bacon bases.

We were in the vicinity of Chichester, at Major Bertram's. His wife, Barbara, was auburn, of course, and she was very gracious. She was constantly busy, from the cellar to the attic, without ever losing her angelic smile and would not not rest until we had something for dinner despite the late hour, or early hour, three o'clock, four o'clock, I didn't know anymore. Bertram, like a Dr. Watson waiting for a Sherlock Holmes, would lend an ear against the door leading into the hall where I could hear whispers, multiple feet climbing the stairs. He was coming back to us, lighting his pipe with scents of exotic wood, and returned again.

— We are not the only ones of our kind here? I finally said to Richards.

— Of course not, Poz. There are others who come and go like you. The key is that you do not meet each others. By the way, he added hastily swallowing his tea, give me now a cover name so that I can have ID papers made for you.

What name do you choose on this side?

— What for? My real name, of course.

— No way. Nobody should be able to spot you.

I was completely bewildered.

— What have I got to fear, here in England?

— Nothing special, but you never know: a spy from the opposite side, an agent in competition with you and with bad intentions.

— You are not logical in this country. In France, I send sentences on the BBC to make believe I'm in England, and, once I'm there, we want to make believe I'm someone else!

— It's like that, he said laconically.

— He drew a cardboard paper and a pen from his pocket. Another identity, the twelfth, the thirteenth, the fourteenth ... Which one was I going to borrow?

— Villeneuve, I said, this is the birthplace of my father, Villeneuve-sur-Yonne.

— Madame de Villeneuve-sur-Yonne? he said somewhat surprised.

— No, just Villeneuve, I love this place. Marie de Villeneuve.

The breakfast ended while pink was coloring the East and the first birds were chirping.

— I'll show you your rooms, said Barbara.

The Major stopped her in her tracks.

— One minute. As I do not know if I'll see you all tomorrow morning, I recommend two things: do not tell anyone, I do specify, anyone, how you came to this country and do not give our address under any circumstances. We do not know, he insisted heavily.

I was taken aback.

— How am I supposed to have arrived here?

— By boat, by plane, via North Africa, in any way except by Lysander.

— But in France, everyone knows it exists, said Poulard. We are even sometimes larging it about the Lysander!

— Not in England, said the major, in a dignified manner. There is not an inhabitant of this country, except a few insiders, who know about it. In my small town of Chichester, nothing is known about what happens at home on full moon nights.

— Even our son, said Barbara. They sleep in the garden in the bread oven.

Above and below.
John Nesbitt-Dufort's Lysander after its crash near Issoudun on 28 January 1942 during Operation « Beryl ». It was ferrying Roger Mitchell "Brick", Maurice Duclos "Saint Jacques" and Julius Kleeberg "Tudor".
(Jean-Michel Rémy collection)

THE DIFFERENT TYPES OF LANDING STRIP MARKING
Landing strips and flashlight markings

Above.
**DZ marking
(norwegian drawing)**
(J-L Perquin)

Below.
**Lysander landing strip
marking (from the
booknote of a French
Veteran).**

IN THE EARLY DAYS, only agents would be parachuted and they would be dropped « Blind » (i.e without any marking on the ground). This procedure was operationaly more secure because it could not lead to any compromission with agents on the ground but it was riskier in the fact that the agent had no idea of the strength and direction of the wind and it was also less accurate. Moreover, if the agent got injured on landing, there was no possibility of him behing immediately taken care of. Thus, the SOE rapidly developed procedures to mark DZs and Pick-up landing strips.

Clandestine landing strips (Pick-up or extraction)

The first ever clandestine landing strip marking was carried out in support of the first Lysander Pick-up (19-20 of October 1940, see at the beginning of this book for more details). The concept had been devised and drawn by the pilot himself, Captain W. J. Farley, on a paper tablecloth of the Oddenino's restaurant.

The landings were invariably carried out at night on landing strips that had previously been inventoried, evaluated and validated by the RAF. The pilot would mostly navigate using ground references (roads, railways, large cities, rivers and lakes) which made those flights reliant on weather and moon conditions. In the final approach phase, the pilot would visualise the landing strip thanks to the landing lights that would then have been switched on by specialy trained

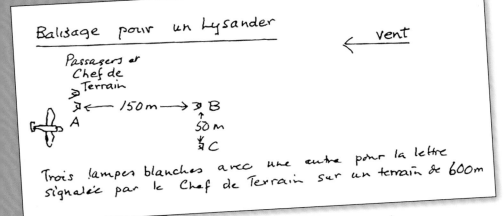

Balisage pour un Lysander — vent

Passagers et Chef de Terrain

←— 150m —→ B
A   50 m
          C

Trois lampes blanches avec une autre pour la lettre signalée par le Chef de Terrain sur un terrain de 600m

Résistance fighters belonging to the reception committee. The procedure remained valid for the duration of the war without major changes (three white flashlights plus a flashlight for the Morse code signal).

Landing strip selection

The landing strip had to be flat. The best option was to choose a ploughed and levelled field. In order to be validated, the landing strip had to be farther away than 5 km to any point higher than 150 metres, have no anti-aircraft position within an 8 km radius and have no tree taller than 10 m in the immediate 300 m around the landing strip. Spotting the landing strip had to be easy for the pilot and landmarks such as a coastline, a railway, or even a straight stretch of road was to be used as long as they would not lead to confusion. When using treelines, great care had to be applied because they could have been modified since the beginning of the war. If the landing strip was on a line between two towns, it could be a good landmark. High ridges were to be avoided.

A message was sent to London with the following information: grid coordinates, altitude, bearing once on the ground (pick-up), length, type of ground, slope (if any), neighbouring obstacles, etc…

Landing strip coordinates

Michelin maps had to be used. The fold which was used was divided into 1 km squares. The top line was given letters from L to Z and the column was given figures from 11 to 30 starting by L and 11.

The following information were then sent by a radio message:

1. Code Name
2. Number of the Michelin map
3. Number of the fold of the Michelin map
4. Bearing to the nearest town of importance
5. Grid coordinates
6. Morse code letter (any letter except TIMESHOV)
7. BBC message (sentence and corresponding code names)

Above.
Lysander landing strip marking as seen from the pilot's position in the cockpit.
(Now it can be told, 1946)

Below.
Sketch of a Hudson landing strip marking (from the booknote of a French Veteran).

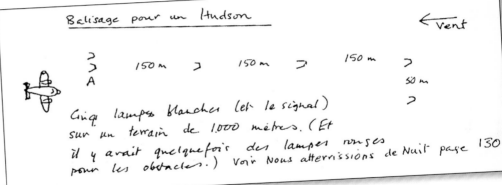

The air drop

The sequence was always the same: the containers, then the agents, then the packets. The containers were dropped every 1/10 of a seconde which meant they were spaced between 5 to 10 m.
- Agents were spaced about 60 m on landing
- The first container was dropped exactly over the second flashlight at an altitude of 150 m.
- Example: 6 agents–6 containers – 2 packets required an area of a minimum of 600 m x 600 m
- The speed and direction of the wind had to be taken into account since trees could for example interfere in the recovery operations.
- Packets were often more difficult to recover. Being lighter, they were blown further away by the wind. The containers weighted 150 kg, requesting six men to man-handle a C Type; five men were enough for an H Type.

Markings

Markings were emplaced two hours before the scheduled arrival of the airplanes and left in place for another two hours after, for five nights in a row. The flashlights had to be left on as long as the airplane was heard. The Morse code letter emitting flashlight had to be pointed 15° in front of the airplane's position and it had to send its code letter very slowly and for as long as the airplane was circling so it could find the exact location of the landing strip.

Para drop markings (beginning of the war)

After the very first marking which had been carried out during the night of the 10th to the 11th of October 1941 near Bergerac (see previous chapter on the Whitley), a standard operating procedure was put in place. Three men with white flashlights were placed at the tips of an equilateral triangle with one angle pointing in the direction of the wind. The man pointing in the direction of the wind also carried a red flashlight emitting a Morse code letter which meant that this was the correct DZ and that it was secured. The airplane dropped its load as it flew over the red and white flashlight so that the force of the wind would then push the parachutes towards the base of the triangle.

Markings for final para drop (transcription from a « Jedburgh » course notes)
Three red flashlight in a row 100 m one from the other
One white flashlight (D) 10m left of the flashlight exposed to the wind; this is the one which emits the morse code letter.

Below.
DZ marking sketch.

Bottom.
Winter DZ marking (Norwegian drawing)
(J-L Perquin)

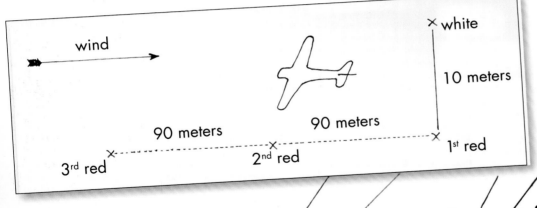

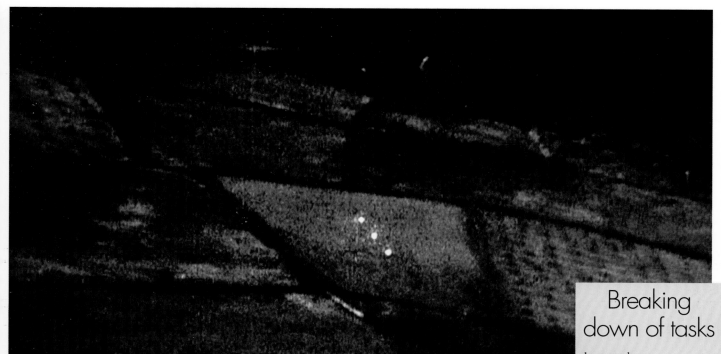

The airplanes arrives on « D » and drops its containers over the second red flashlight.

Wind estimate for a 150 m (500 ft) para drop:

	Drift	Handkerchief
8 kph	60 m	15°
16 kph	120 m	30°
24 kph	180 m	55°
32 kph	240 m	80°

Compute the location of the flashlights according to those data. For example, with a 24 kph wind, the second red = length of the containers + drift from a container + drift for one man.

Composition of the reception committee

Operational security: the less, the better (unless you are with a Maquis)

Manhandling:

1 container ≠ 150 kg = 4 men

Camouflage: holes have to be dug in advance in order to bury the containers

Example: 6 containers x 4 men + 2 lookouts + 1 commander = 27 men, that's already a lot of people!

The containers

The containers and the packets will be the subject of an in-depth study in a yet-to-be-released book.

C Type: cylindrical in shape, 1,80 m long, opening from top to bottom, rubber shock absorbers at the base. Attached to the 500 lbs bomb launchers and linked by a static line, a small « pilot » parachute allows a quick opening of the main canopy. This « pilot » parachute often comes undone (1 m sleeve): you need to look for them

H Type: 1,70 m, 5 cells, iron construction, iron shock absorber (normally gets crushed), housing for the parachute on top, shovel on the side like the C Type, hooks for the parachute's risers. Opens by removing the cells, each cell having a shock absorbing ring and a carrying handle. The cell has a top opening (mind the piece of string which is used as a seal). Do not leave anything behind you: 5 pins, 5 rings, 5 straps, 2 locks….

Above.
DZ marking as seen from the pilot's position in the cockpit.
(Now it can be told, 1946)

Below.
Sketch of a Lysander landing strip marking.

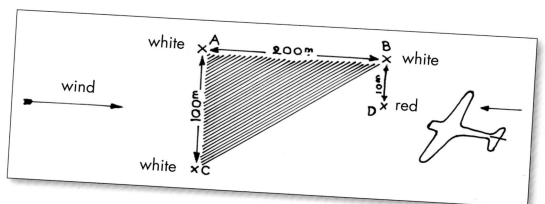

Above.
Lysander landing strip marking as seen from the ground.
(Now it can be told, 1946)

Below.
Triangle-shape DZ marking. (Beginning of the war).

A cardboard-based container which would be easy to burn is currently under study.

Paratroops containers (CLE) can sometimes be found: they look like the C type.

Packets
Outside packing
Radio set: wrapped in the team's clothes.

Agents
Do not leave the rubber helmet, the cushion or the overall on the strip.

NB: on each container, a sticker indicates the number of containers and packets. (example 12 P4 = 12 containers and 4 packets).

Specific markings:
Red triangle: radio equipment
CO: Chief Ops
DM: Délégué Militaire (Military delegate)
SPE: Spéciale (Special Demolition)
CR: Comité de réception (reception committee)
Packets A 500: suitcases of the parachuted agents

Strip No 3: Renard (La Baume–Mont¬Billiat)
Marking: 3 large wood fires in the shape of an equilateral triangle with a 100 metres base. One tip of the triangle is in the direction of the wind and, 50 to 80 metres in the axis of this tip, a white flashlight sends the indicated Morse code letter.

As soon as the noise of the plane is heard, light the fires (it is recommended to pour some petrol on the fire before lighting it up for better results) and, with the flashlight, send the code letter in Morse very slowly and very deliberately.

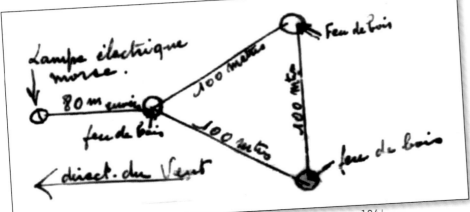

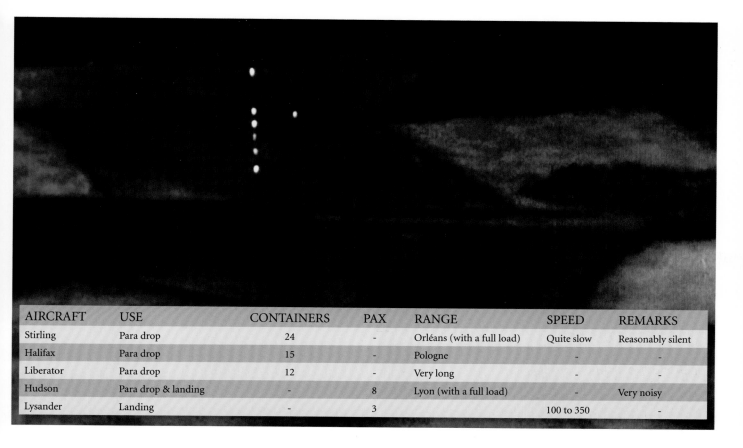

AIRCRAFT	USE	CONTAINERS	PAX	RANGE	SPEED	REMARKS
Stirling	Para drop	24	-	Orléans (with a full load)	Quite slow	Reasonably silent
Halifax	Para drop	15	-	Pologne	-	-
Liberator	Para drop	12	-	Very long	-	-
Hudson	Para drop & landing	-	8	Lyon (with a full load)	-	Very noisy
Lysander	Landing	-	3		100 to 350	-

Keep on « Morsing » until the operation is well underway and repeat the process if other airplanes arrive (see the sketch above).

Message: « The fox is in the chicken coop » is broadcasted on the BBC at 16 : 30, 19 : 30 and 21 : 15 hours. Make sure two different sets will be listening to this broadcast at the above mentioned times and during the moon period dated 28 May to 9 June included.

Morse code letter: R ; the operation will be executed on the night the message will be broadcasted, between 00 : 30 and 03 : 30 hours.

The marking team should be in place no later than 23 : 30 hours.

General orders: It is possible that the message will be broadcasted on a possible evening but that no aircraft shows up, for any given reason. If this happens, listen again to the BBC broadcast the next day and the following evenings until the end of the moon phase.

The operation can resume 1, 2, 3 or 4 days later during the above mentioned dates. An operation which has been postponed in that way will always be announced by a broadcast on the same evening. It is of the utmost importance that complete secrecy

be maintained on the message and on its meaning. Only people with a need to know will listen to it and they will not know its exact meaning unless it is absolutely necessary. The reception commitee will not know the message.

If the operation is a success, immediatly conceal all the equipment which has been dropped, remove all traces of activity and immediatly report with all the necessary details and accuracy to the local leader. In case of a failure, report in the same way. Never forget that for an operation to be successful, the above mentioned procedures must be followed. The sender will be all the more motivated to drop more supplies if they feel the reception committee is working smoothly and is up to the task. It will be easier to perform more operations if the first one is a success.

Strip No I: Pig (Chèvrerie)
Message: « Les petits cochons sont gras. » (The piglets are fat)
Morse letter: P.

Strip No 2: Wolf (Memises)
Message: The wolf wanders in the woods.
Morse letter: L

Above.
Hudson landing strip marking as seen from the pilot's position in the cockpit.
(Now it can be told, 1946)

Morse letter: L

The regional SAP commander to all his team leaders

Transmitted by the départemental SAP commander of Haute-Savoie (Paulain)

Any and all DZ team leader must be capable of conducting on his own the reception of an operation. Difficulties in getting from one point to another mean that a team leader can be forced to carry out an operation without his départemental commander being present. Some teams have already performed very well under such circumstances. Still, we feel that it is necessary to remind everybody of the standard operating procedures for para drops as well as of some general orders.

Before the operation

The team must only be made up of tried and tested men : 10 to 15 is enough.

Chatterboxes and drunkards have to be culled from your teams. Only the team commander, his second in command and two or three men must know the messages. For security reasons, our messages cannot be known by everybody.

Among the team members, only the commander and his second in command must know the Morse-code letter identifying the landing strip and be capable of operating the flashlight.

The team commander and his second in command must be able to operate the Eureka device if the départemental commander has brought it to the landing strip.

Always keep a set of spare red and white flashlights and spare batteries.

Prepare in advance 3 or 4 « stretchers » made up of four pieces of wood tied together in order to facilitate the movements of the containers.

Never move your field to another location, even for security reasons, without giving prior notice to your départemental commander.

Make sure the cache your intend to use is available around the clock.

The messages are broadcasted at 13 : 30, 19 : 30 and 21 : 15 hours. Depending on whether the message is repeated during the 21 : 30 broadcast or not, the operation is confirmed or cancelled. It may happen that in spite of the broadcast being repeated at 21 : 15 hours, the operation does not take place. The airplane may have encountered all sort of difficulties : mechanical breakdown, severe weather, flak, enemy fighter.

Make sure you always have transportation assets with you.

The operation per se.

Be on your position as soon as 23 : 00 hours. Wait for the airplane until 3300 hours.

The team will be broken down in three separate elements :

the team leader and three men will be in charge of the marking ;

an armed team will provide security on the outskirts of the landing strip ;

The rest of the team will be positioned all around the strip.

No small talks, no cigarette while the plane is expected.

A German or a Gendarmerie patrol could pass by and overhear or see you.

For the duration of the operation, determine a password for all the personnel operating on the strip or who could need to go across it.

The red flashlights marked R1 R2 R3 are approximatively 80 metres from one another ; the B white flashlight which will send the Morse letter is 3 metres from the first red flashlight. The plane always comes opposite the wind : the white flashlight is thus in close proximity to the first flashlight that the plane will see.

Switch the Eureka on as early as midnight.

Switch the flashlights on as soon as the plane arrives over the strip. It will circle the landing strip two or three times before dropping its load.

The use of Eureka does not preclude the use of flashlights.

Sometimes, the plane will drop its load in two passes ; the marking must thus not be moved unless you are sure all the drops have been done and the plane is heading back.

The broadcast of the Morse-code letter is vital : some drops were cancelled because the letter had not been broadcasted.

Count the parachutes when they are in the air and pinpoint the place where they have fallen.

After the operation

The security team should not be involved in the recovery of the containers. Its must focus on its mission which is to guard the landing site.

Never remove first the parachute and then the containers. If the night is dark, the parachute will help you to locate the containers.

Remove all traces of your activities on the landing strip. Normally, a large white sticker with a black figure on it indicate the total number of containers released during the drop. In all cases, a team member will walk the strip early in the morning in order to insure nothing has been left there.

Make sure nothing gives your equipment cache away. If the equipment has to stay there for a while, do not hang around the cache. If you need to establish a guard element, make sure it is of a discreet nature.

The team commander should not distribute the equipment. The kit which has arrived is not necessarily all for you : it is for the Résistance as a whole. Nevertheless, the team commander is responsible for this equipment until it is allocated. The inventory of the equipment will only be done in the presence of the départemental commander of the SAP.

Under no condition should the cells marked with C.O. or with a red triangle on a white square or with a black letter S on a round, red background should be opened. These cells will be directly handed over by the Regional Command to specific addressees that London will designate directly.

It is stressed that the teams should be capable of completely autonomous operations. A day will come, and it may come very soon, when all liaison will be impossible and our movements will be almost completely restricted. It is important that even in such conditions, receptions can still be carried out. The supply drops will be used to arm the area into which they have landed. As a consequence, the team should be made up of people living close to the landing strips.

The team leaders and their second in command must know perfectly well the standard operating procedures as well as all the intelligence pertaining to the landing strip they are responsible for such as messages, Morse-code letter etc.

The teams must alays have a few spare flashlights. In case of need, wood fires can be used instead as indicated in the standard operating procedures.

In case of a landing, the teams must be on permanent alert status without waiting for a forewarning from the départemental commander. This means that BBC broadcasts should be permanently listened to.

161 Squadron's Lysander Mk III SD JR « M » R 9125 (JR : April 1944 to 1945) in its final approach before landing. This plane is currently on show at the RAF museum in Hendon and is the last remaining 161 Squadron airplane. Unfortunately, it is missing its external long-range tank. The ladder has been repainted in the Army camouflage pattern. On the other hand, the rear cockpit is still in the SD version. (Now it can be told, 1946)

THE S-PHONE (secret telephone)

DURING CLANDESTINE PARACHUTE OPERATIONS, it is highly recommended to establish a link between the ground and the air element. The first prototypes of a signal equipment capable of offering such capabilities were trialled as early as October 1940 in Great-Britain. The specifications of this clandestine system were as such: it had to be compact, light and discreet; the range

Left.
Notebook belonging to Capitaine Jean Souquet a.k.a « Kernevel »; he used it while following his Jedburgh training in Milton Hall. Those specific pages deal with the B 2 suitcase and the S-Phone. Capitaine Souquet jumped at the head of the « Felix » team on 9 July 1944 near Jugon in the Cotes du Nord département..
(Bertrand Souquet collection)

could be limited to line-of-sight and an additional layer of security would be provided by the fact the system would only emit a narrow wave beam, just like an invisible ray of light. The use of ultra-short waves, just like in Radars, offered the solution to this technical problem. Thus, clandestine operators could rely on an unsecure, real-time radio-telephone connectivity from 1943 onwards. The device itself, which was very light, was strapped to the body of the signaller. The aerial, made up of two vertical branches for a total length of about 60 cm, was placed 25 cm in front of the chest of the signaller.

Fitted with an efficient headset and a microphone with a wrap-around mouthpiece, both the signals coming from the aircraft and the messages sent by the ground operator were impossible to intercept by anybody standing near. The S-Phone transceiver used a « duplex » system which meant that it went from « emit » to « receive » without having to perform any specific operation, just like with an ordinary telephone.

Its range varied, depending on the operating conditions. A high flying plane heading straight for a ground operator could establish contact up to 60 km away. The signaller having to face the direction of the arriving plane, he had to be assisted by another member of the reception committee who would « steer » him towards the incoming sound by placing his hands on the signaller's shoulders. Thus, the practical range would fall to roughly 15 km. The radio emissions of the incoming airplanes could not be detected by any ground stations located over 1,500 metres from the origin point.

During the radio communication, mutual identification was insured by code-phrases

(continued on page 113)

Above.
S-phone transceiver in a plane.
*(*Now it can be told, 1946)

Right.
The S-Phone in details depicting the various components of this air to ground system.
(Georges Ricard collection)

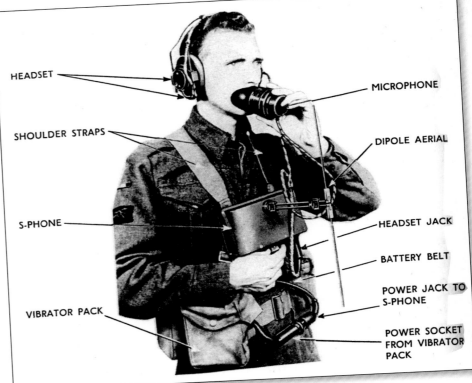

HEADSET

MICROPHONE

SHOULDER STRAPS

DIPOLE AERIAL

S-PHONE

HEADSET JACK

BATTERY BELT

POWER JACK TO S-PHONE

VIBRATOR PACK

POWER SOCKET FROM VIBRATOR PACK

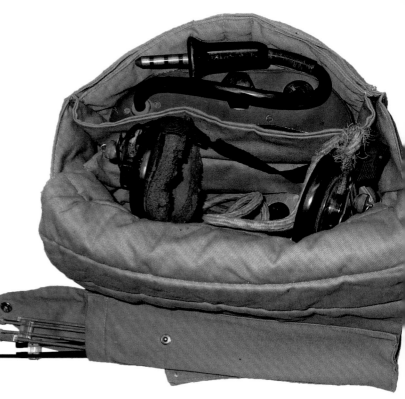

Paul Rivière (1946) alias « Marquis » was parachuted in as an emergency measure 21 July 1943 on the « Vincent » DZ in Cormatin (Saône et Loire département) in order to take commande of the section des atterrissages et parachutages (landing and para drops section) for the Southern Zone. He personaly controled 13 clandestine Pick-ups. Recalled to London in May 1944, he was once again parachuted in the Saône et Loire département on 7 June 1944 during Operation « John 87 A » on the « Metacarpe » DZ ion Soulcy near the river Arroux, close to the city of Gueugnon.
(Centre d'Histoire de la Résistance et de la Déportation, Lyon)

Above, left and below.
Paul Rivière's S-phone Mk III pouch is held in a stuffed bag of a seldom seen type.
(J-L Perquin, Centre d'Histoire de la Résistance et de la Déportation, Lyon)

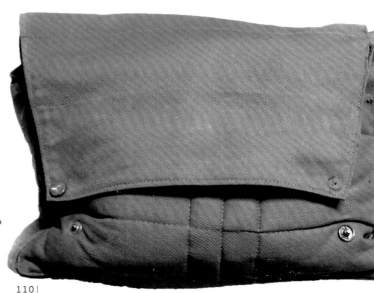

Operator's Manual

Pre-operation checks:
- Acid level; if necessary, add cold boiled water
- Contact between the batteries
- Vibrator (slight purring)
- Connect the different elements
- Caution, when opening the box, wave length are changed

If the set is unserviceable, destroy it with ½ lbs of plastic explosive and request another set.

Assembly:
- Put the belt on and check the operation of the vibrator (slight purring)
- Place the set on the suspenders of the web belt (vibrator in the OFF position)
- Place the aerial and the headset
- Plug in the set and the aerial and then the vibrator; after a slight pause a hissing sound can be heard in the headset; (if not, jolt the jacks): the transceiver is now on. Check that the aerial are in a vertical position with the help of a handkerchief (that's what works best).
- Slide two wet fingers on top of the aerial while softly whistling into the microphone; it is heard in the headset: the transceiver is operational.
- NB: do not plug the set to the batteries if the transceiver has not been fully assembled.

Operation:
Get on the air a few moments before the aircraft is due and turned towards the sector it is supposed to arrive from; make sure there are no obstacle between the aircraft and the S-phone operator. Signals are strongest 6° above the horizontal. Swiftly turn the knob until the communication with the aircraft is as clear as possible. Then stop moving unless the volume is too loud when the aircraft is too close. When the aircraft signals, the hissing sound disappears, do not touch the setting knob. When the aircraft is overhead, follow it.

Recharging:
- 190-250 V generator
- When recharging: generator on OFF and battery vents opened
- Recharge during 24 hours on the 1 Ampere setting, two days before the operation
- When no operation are scheduled: recharge for 24 hours once a week
- Always keep the batteries in the vertical position (because of the acid).

Right.
Two Résistance fighters perform a daylight, post-war re-enactement of the use of an S-Phone. The assistant helps the operator to face the incoming aircraft by pressing on his shoulder in a pre-arranged manner.
(SHD)

Range:
- The aircrafts fitted with the most powerful sets can hear the S-Phone 30 km away.
- The S-phone can establish contact with the aircraft 10 to 15 km away.

Advices:
- Avoid main obstacles such as high-voltage cables, electric railways, telephone cables etc…
- Place the operator at least 10 metres from another man and behind the head of the reception committee. The ground wave length is ¾ at 1 km which means that one would need two Direction Finding sets less than one kilometre away to locate and pinpoint the S-Phone. Only an aircraft can achieve that with relative ease.

Procedure:
Aircraft: *Hello Garbo, here is a tunning call*
Ground element: *Hello Carole, I hear you loud an clear*
Aircraft: *Hello Garbo, I hear you loud and clear, I have a message for you*
Ground element: *pass your message*
Aircraft: *I have 5 containers, 3 men, 2 packets for you*
Ground element: *I understand you have 5 containers, 3 men, 2 packets for me*
Aircraft: *That is correct, Here they come*
Ground element: *1, 2, 3, 4, 5….. I have received 5 containers, 3 men, 2 packets*

Right.
Drawing of the S-Phone as it was supposed to be worn:
A S-phone
B Power jack to S-phone
C Headset
D Headset and microphone audio cables
E Microphone
F Headset and microphone audio cables
G Headset and microphone jack
K Antenna jack
H T-shaped dipole aerial
L Power socket from vibrator pack
M Web harness
N Vibrator pack

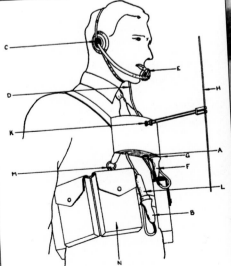

François Delimal
a.k.a: Jacques Fontaine—Faraday — Gouverneur

François Delimal was born in Paris on 16 February 1922. His father was a French Navy Officer.

A student at the renowned Lycée Louis-le-Grand in Paris and then at the elite Ecole des Sciences Politiques also in Paris, he was also a university boxing champion. In 1942, he was recruited by the « Organisation Nationale de la Résistance » movement. In Epernay, in the Marne département, François Delimal developed a new group within this organisation. Tasked with the liaison with the Bureau des Opérations Aériennes (BOA, Air Operations Bureau), and as deputy to Michel Pichard, a.k.a « Pic », he carried out several intelligence gathering missions, transported weapons, organised radio networks, resupply drops and Pick-up operations.

He left for London in September 1943 and underwent some specialized training. Six weeks later, during the night of the 16th to the 17th of October 1943, he was parachuted with a saboteur, Jean Jolivet (a.k.a Barque), on DZ « Musset » near Cormoyeux, North East of Epernay in the Champagne département. He was not yet 22 of age but still, he was tasked with the organisation of all para drops in the C Region which comprised the Haute-Marne, Marne, Côte d'Or et Haute-Saône département. He was to confirm dozens of DZs and to validate their reception committees. François Delimal was arrested with his deputies by the Gestapo on 20 March 1944 in rue de Lourmel, the Paris base of the BOA.

Taken to the Gestapo torture centre of the rue des Saussaies in Paris, he committed suicide 21 March 1944 during an interrogation with a cyanide pill which he had been given in London.

He was made a Compagnon de la Libération by a 28 May 1945 decree.

Type W.S. 13/3 S-phone in its case. This particular set was operated by François Delimal, a Compagnon de la Libération, who received it during the night of the 17th of September 1943 on the « Musset » DZ which was run by the Epernay section of the Bureau des opérations aériennes (BOA).
(J-L Perquin, Musée de l'Ordre de la Libération)

and by the « nom de guerre » given to each of the local leaders. The airplane would receive information from the ground such as the wind speed and direction as well as all the necessary details on the weather.

When S-phones transceivers were used to establish contact between an emissary from London and the heads of networks on the ground, the airplane would fly around in circle in order to remain inside the « emision cone ». Onboard the aircraft, the S-phone broadcast was connected to the intercom and this sometimes led to some interesting situations. During an operation in the Bordeaux area, a tail-gunner reported he could see the landing lights of the reception committee and that they were « bloody pathetic »…after a few seconds, the S-Phone of the ground party answered: " And how would your landing lights be if the Gestapo was less than two kilometres away?"

A naval version of the S-phone was produced at the beginning of 1944 in order to support clandestine landing and extraction of men and equipment. When adding the three areas of operations (Mediterranean Sea, Atlantic and the Channel), it is estimated that a total of 3,000 passengers were exfiltrated and another 1,500 infiltrated with naval assets. The discrepancy between the exfiltration and the infiltration figures can be explained by the fact that escape « rat lines » used naval assets more than any other.

The naval S-Phone had inverted frequencies and they only were issued following a specific request. A green dot on the set indicated a normal S-phone and an orange dot indicated a dual-use set which, after a change of aerial and lamps, could revert to air communications.

Peculiar uses of the S-phone, two SOE F stories

Capitaine Henri Paul Sevenet (Rodolphe or Mathieu, a.k.a Capitaine H. Thomas), head of the « Détective » network conducted several missions in occupied France. On his third mission, he was dropped « Blind » on 15 September 1943 in order to create a new network in the Aude and Ariège départements. Not having been provided with a dedicated radio operator, on 22 March 1944 he used an S-phone to report to London that he had organized a 200-man strong group in the Montagne Noir area and that he requested further orders as well as weapons drops.

On 20 July 1944, he was killed in action near La Galaube when nearly 1,500 German soldiers supported by aircrafts, artillery, armoured vehicles and tanks attacked his maquis. He was litteraly decapitated by a German bomb. His body was found four days latter, the Germans having dumped it on a manure heap. He was buried with full military honours in the Lafrade cemetary.

Below.
S-Phone type 13 Mk III set in its « naval version ».

Bottom left.
Top view of an S-Phone type 13 Mk III set in its « naval version ». Notice the green dot indicating the normal configuration.
(J-L Perquin, Georges Ducreuzet collection)

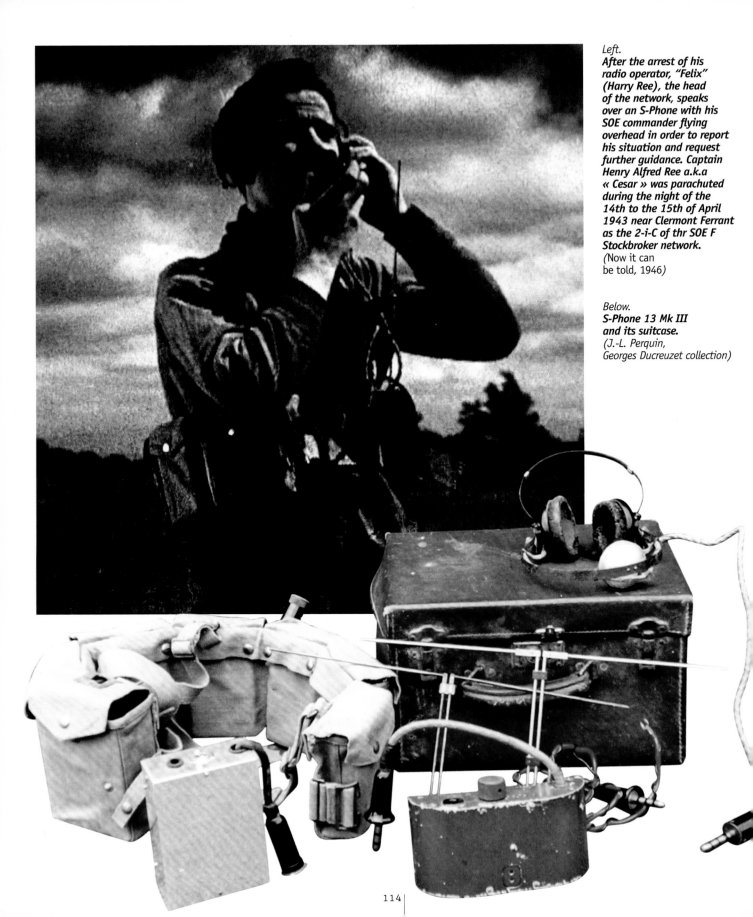

Left.
After the arrest of his radio operator, "Felix" (Harry Ree), the head of the network, speaks over an S-Phone with his SOE commander flying overhead in order to report his situation and request further guidance. Captain Henry Alfred Ree a.k.a « Cesar » was parachuted during the night of the 14th to the 15th of April 1943 near Clermont Ferrant as the 2-i-C of thr SOE F Stockbroker network.
(Now it can be told, 1946)

Below.
S-Phone 13 Mk III and its suitcase.
(J.-L. Perquin,
Georges Ducreuzet collection)

Above and below.
On 14 July 44, Maurice Mercier « Péruvien » who had been recruted in France in early 1942, operates an S-Phone 13 Mk III during Operation « Cadillac » on DZ « Taille-Crayon » (pencil sharpener) located in Vassieux en Vercors. On that day, 72 B17 dropped 862 containers.
(Au cœur de l'orage)

Left.
S-phone Mk III used during the night of the 7th to the 8th of January 1944 in support of the drop of Major Henry Van Maurik a.k.a John Patterson near Izernore-Bussy, 7 km North West of Nantua (Ain).
(Musée d'Histoire de la Résistance et de la Déportation de l'Ain et du Haut-Jura)

Secret ultra high frequency duplex radio telephone system (U.H.F)
Country: United Kingdom
Organisation: SOE
Introduction: 1942 and 1943
Power output: 100 – 200 MW
Belt filled with six batteries (2 Volt each, total 9 hours of operation)
Frequency: 337 MHz
Weight: 9,5 kg (with the felt lined suitcase)
Length of the aerial:
40 cm to 20 cm away from the chest of the operator
Maximum emission/reception range with an aircraft:
at an altitude of 600 m: 16 – 24 Km
at an altitude of 1500 m: 24 – 30 Km
at an altitude of 3000 m: 45 – 60 Km

Emitter/Receiver
height: 15 cm
length: 8,6 cm
width: 22,8 cm
weight: 0,9 kg

Belt with batteries
height: 15 cm
length: 6,3 cm
width: 76 cm
weight: 7,7 kg

Below.
S Phone 13 Mk IV.
(Norwegian Armed Forces Museum
Oslo, Norway)

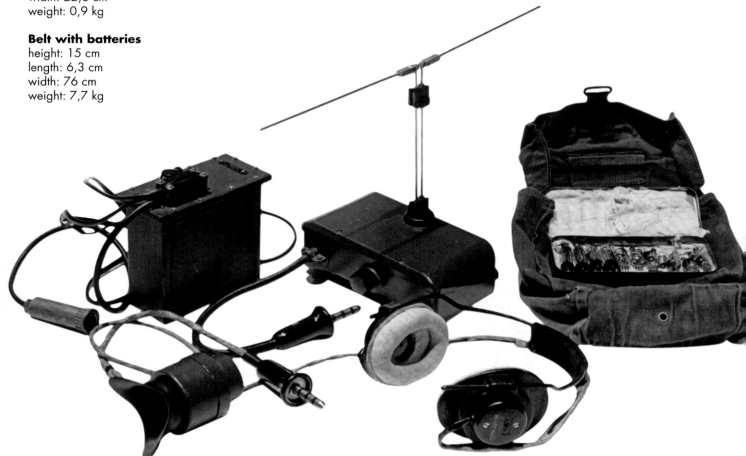

The S-phone was held in place over the belt by two web suspenders. The deployed antenna was plugged to its jack. The radio operator adjusted the frequency control with his right hand in order to get the best possible audio. The web suspenders were attached to the belt which held seven web pouches. Five of those pouches held miniaturised cadmium nickel batteries while the two others held the vibrator power source, the microphone and headset assembly and the folded aerial when the S-phone was not in use.

Destruction

The S-phone would quiclky melt when exposed to a charcoal or wood fuelled fire. The battery belt and the web harness could also be burnt. The microphone and headset could still be identified once they had been burnt so they would have had to be disposed of in deep water or buried. In an emergency, the standard operating procedure was to destroy the S-phone with explosives.

- Remove the S-phone from its web harness and place it on the ground
- Plut the blasting cap on the « G » position of the headset by pushing on it as hard as possible so as to bury it inside the headset.
- Remove the waterproof cover of the head of the blasting cap by pulling on the tab. The paper. enveloppe will fall off.
- Lit up the blasting cap using the provided friction strip or any safety match box.
- Once the fuse is lit, there is a 20 secondes delay to take shelter at least 20 metres away before the cap explodes. Of course, the equipment would never be destroyed while still on the operator....

S-Phone 13
Mk III.
(Musée Radiomili)

The Wheelwright network

INSERTED by naval assets near Cassis at the same time as a large quantity of equipment earmarked for the Marseille reception committee, Major George Reginald Starr (a.k.a Hilaire or Gaston) landed in Southern France from a feluca crewed by Polish sailors on November 8, 1942. At the beginning of April 1943, Starr received two airdrops comprising nine containers and two packets for his own network. One of those drops included an S-phone which would prove extremely useful in July of the same year.

In June 1943, Starr reported via Berne in Switzerland that his group was organized in 10 districts, each with its own commander and headquarters, ready for D-day. At the same time, using his S-phone, he requested London to send him a plane so he could report directly on his progresses and organise further weapons and equipment drops.

This S-phone broadcast took place on 22 July 1943 and it paved the way for a further 147 air operations that delivered 2,069 containers and 553 packets!

He finally received his first radio operator, Yvonne Cormeau (a.k.a Annette or Fairy) during the night of the 22nd to the 23rd of August 1943. The success of the forthcoming 147 parachute drops relied heavily on her. Yvonne Cormeau worked tirelessly until the Liberation, sending more than a record 400 radio messages in extremly demanding conditions.

Another radio operator, Lieutenant Denis Parsons (a.k.a Pierrot) was dropped on 11 April 1944. He sent 84 radio messages and then joined the Maquis after D-day. He was to be slightly wounded during the battle around Castelnau on 21 June 1944.

Latter on, in 1944 and within the frame of the Sussex plan, a special Squadron was created in order to establish direct contacts with the operators on the ground. Some Frenchmen, including the famous reporter and writer Joseph Kessel, would speak directly with ground teams that led close air support airplanes on enemy concentrations of troops and armoured vehicles.

The Sussex sometimes operated in the midst or very close to German units. The experience of William Bechtel a.k.a Bonnet (Sussex / Berthier mission, parachuted during the night of the 8th to the 9th of April 1944 near Neuvy-Pailloux in the Indre département) is worth mentioning. He managed to give « Marius » (Joseph Kessel) real-time intelligence by S-phone throughout the battle of Rouen. Thanks to the S-Phone, he also managed to report the location of V1 sites between Paris and Rouen

as well as to indicate the position of V1 road convoys moving towards Dieppe. Bechtel even managed to pinpoint the exact location of a V1 fuel depot and to indicate the time when it would be filled to capacity; in the morning, he had the satisfaction of seeing two RAF fighter-bombers destroy the target he had indicated, the fuel tanks blowing up one after the other in an orgy of flames that today's Hollywood film makers would be proud of. In an way, he was paving the way for today's JTAC

---

1. JTAC: *Joint Terminal Attack Controller.* An Air Force liaison element working in support of ground forces.

THE EUREKA BEACON

The Rebecca/Eureka transponding radar was a short-range radio navigation system used for the dropping of airborne forces and their supplies.

Eureka would only be activated when it received a pulse sent by a Rebecca placed onboard an incoming aircraft. A low crackling sound would indicate that an airplane had locked on it and that it would soon arrive on the landing strip. On the Rebecca Indicator Unit, the location of the airplane relative to its axis of approach was indicated on a scale of 90, 36 or 9 metres depending on the sensitivity which had been selected by the crew.

The performances of this system made it possible for an aircraft to drop « blind », for example over a layer of fog, with an accuracy of about 50 metres. As early as July

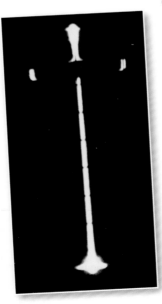

1941, portable Rebecca/Eureka beacons were trialled in order to guide Whitleys towards their DZs. Those trials led to the crash of a Whitley (Z6727) near Newmarket (Suffolk). Rebecca-equipped RAF aircrafts received the Eureka return signal through two directional antennas. On board the aircraft, a Radar screen indicated the distance to the Eureka as well as the location of the aircraft relative to the axis defined by the beacon. An additional antenna made it possible to compute the distance separating the emitter from the receiver. The theoretical range of the system was supposed to be in the vicinity of 130 km (80 miles) if the plane flew at an altitude of 200 metres. Initially, the Eureka was packed in a heavy and bulky case; it then was improved and fitted into a bergen. The system was battery-powered and its antenna, composed of three pieces, was four metres high. Because the technologies employed in the Eureka were highly secret and unknown to the Germans, the system

was fitted with an explosive self-destruction device in order to insure it could not be studied in depth in case it was to fall into enemy hands. At the end of 1943, some dropping zones, known as «depots» were equipped with Eureka. The systems were switched on every night during the full moon period (between the first and the last quarters). When they had been unable to locate their intended DZs, this allowed some aircrafts to come and drop their loads on those alternate zones rather than bring them back to the UK.

Operating constraints: the Eureka system had to be placed close to the central lamp of the DZ marking and it had to be more than 50 metres away from any isolated tree, 150 metres away from any house, telephone lines or treeline (300 metres away if the trees were taller than 10 metres) and more than 250 metres from high-tension cables. Deep valley were not recommended as no summit higher than 150 metres was allowed within a 5 km radius. It could be moved to 500 metres to be placed on a high and cleared ground. No anti-aircraft position was allowed in a 8 km (5 miles) radius.

Later on, Eureka was also used as a simple beacon marking out air routes for night or low visibility flights. Any bomber overflying a Eureka-covered route

could thus readjust its bearing. Unless the RAF stated otherwise, the system was operating every single night. Its identification was achieved through the continuous Morse-code broadcast of two letters. Those two letters changed nightly according to a pre-determined list.

For example, a memo dated 26 May 1944 ordered «Marquis» (Rivière) to emplace a Eureka beacon codenamed «Margatte» on a line drawn between Grenoble and Valence as close as possible to the village of La Chapelle. It had to be oriented West-South West as well as North as much as possible. This beacon had to be permanently active and only switched off when the code phrase «Margot cueille des marguerites» (Margot is picking daisies) was broadcasted by the BBC. The operators of that particular system were warned that they would often had to guide planes that would not be operating in their direct support.

In 1947, during the Arctic expeditions of the Expéditions Polaires Françaises led by Paul-Emile Victor, the base located in the geometrical centre of the Groenland–76° Northing – used a « Eureka-Beacon » to guide the B 24 tasked with its parachute resupply. The range of the beacon signals was no more than one hundred of the 2,720 kilometres that separated Keflavik from the polar station.

Country: United Kingdom
Organisation: SOE, resistance movements
Manufacturer: Master Radio
Introduction: 1944
Power output: 10-12 W
Emitter and receiver: Type TR 3164
Emission Frequency Band: 213,5 MHz
Reception Frequency Band: 217,5 MHz
Power source: type 289
Aerial: type 157

Above.
Eureka Mk I beacon used
for training in an SOE STS
(Special Training School)
somewhere in the UK.
(Now it can be told, 1946)

   This type was used as a basis for further development but it only was produced for resistance movements from 1944 on. Delivered in a wooden crate, the whole set was quite heavy: the beacon weighed 7.3 kg, the power source weighed 5 kg and the batteries added another 4 kg. Cadnium-Nickel batteries provided 7 hours of operation. The antenna had a characteristic « T » shape. This set achieved some good results in France.

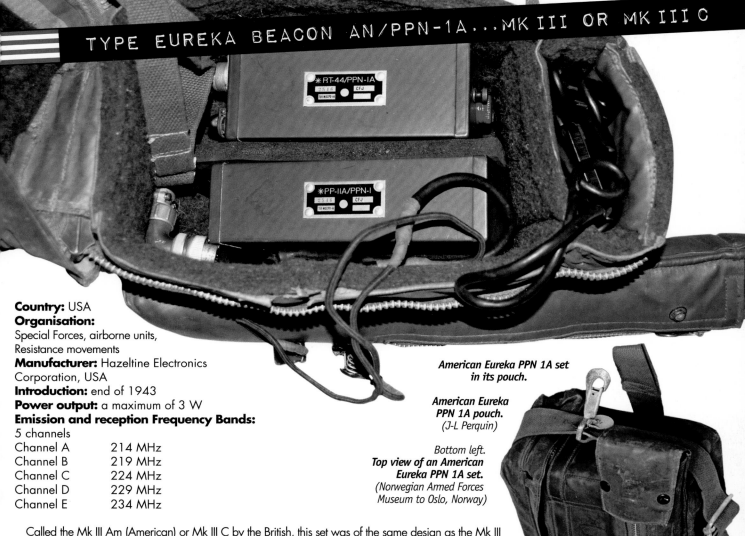

Country: USA
Organisation:
Special Forces, airborne units,
Resistance movements
Manufacturer: Hazeltine Electronics
Corporation, USA
Introduction: end of 1943
Power output: a maximum of 3 W
Emission and reception Frequency Bands:
5 channels

Channel A	214 MHz
Channel B	219 MHz
Channel C	224 MHz
Channel D	229 MHz
Channel E	234 MHz

*American Eureka PPN 1A set
in its pouch.*

*American Eureka
PPN 1A pouch.*
(J-L Perquin)

Bottom left.
**Top view of an American
Eureka PPN 1A set.**
*(Norwegian Armed Forces
Museum to Oslo, Norway)*

Called the Mk III Am (American) or Mk III C by the British, this set was of the same design as the Mk III but it was produced in the United States. More sophisticated but also more fragile than the British version, it required meticulous care in its handling. The set fitted in a canvas or a rubberized bag.

This set, the American version of the British Eureka Mk II is also known as the Mk II C. It was developed in close cooperation with the British in 1943. A rubber knob located on the right of the antenna cable on the RT-44/PPN-1A can be used to manually send a letter in Morse code in order to identify the operator to the incoming aircraft. Originaly intended for the american airborne divisions, the SOE nevertheless dropped a quite considerable amount of those sets to the Résistance movements to supplement the two British types. Just like the British version, the American set was fitted with an explosive charge located in the back of the transceiver in order to destroy it in case of an imminent capture.

Emitter/Receiver
height: 22 cm   length: 11 cm
width: 7 cm   weight: 1,4 kg

RT-44/PPN-1A
Power source
height: 22 cm   length: 11 cm
width: 6 cm   weight: 2 kg

PP-11A/PPN-1
Complete set in its transit case
height: 46 cm   length: 26 cm
width: 19 cm   weight: 14,5 kg

Type AS-83/PPN-1A
antenna on a 2.7 m mast

Type CY-77/PPN 1A Batteries

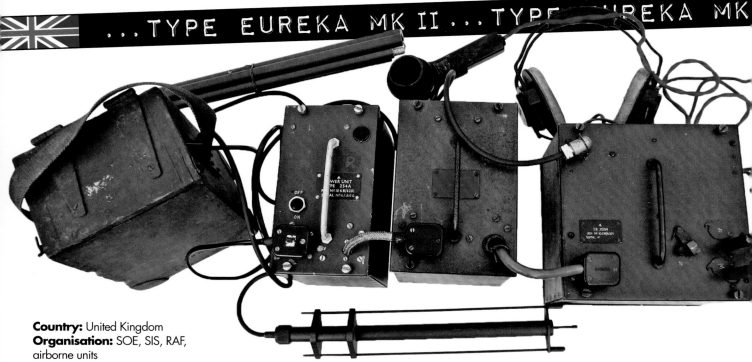

Country: United Kingdom
Organisation: SOE, SIS, RAF, airborne units
Manufacturer: Murphy Radio
Introduction: 1943
Power output: 10-12 W;12 volts with for hours of operation
Emission and reception Frequency Bands: 5 channels

Channel A	214 MHz
Channel B	219 MHz
Channel C	224 MHz
Channel D	229 MHz
Channel E	234 MHz

It was used for DZ marking by the Résistance but its weight and size meant that most operators prefered to use the MkI and Mk IIIB sets.

Above.
Eureka Mk II F set with its folded Type 304A antenna. From left to right: Type 254A power cable, Type 51A code book and TR 3559 transceiver.
(Pierret collection)

Below.
Eureka Mk II set, TR 3174 transceiver (Muséeradiomili collection and picture). K: (Key) morse code broadcast; N: (Noise) test switch; P: (Phones) plug for the jack of the reception headset; M: (Meter) length test in metres; T: Transmitter channel selector; R: Receiver channel selector; D: Detonator socket for selfdestruction; A: Antenna plug
(SHD)

Emitter/Receiver
height: 18 cm
length: 20,5 cm
width: 20,5 cm
weight: 2,8 kg

TYPE TR 3174
Power source
height: 18 cm
length: 11,5 cm
width: 20,5 cm
weight: 3,3 kg

TYPE 254 OR 254 A
Nickel-iron batttery
height: 19 cm
length: 29 cm
width: 14 cm
weight: 10 kg

Type 304A antenna
weight: 1,8 kg

Transit case
height: 25,4 cm
length: 49,5 cm
width: 33 cm
weight: 7,7 kg

TYPE 107
antenna lenght
(vertical on tripod): 2,7 m

Memo from the Air Ministry dated April 1943

The use of Rebecca – Eureka sets being limited by their single channel, the new Mk II version now opens the multichannel capability on 5 channels each separated by 5 Hz between 214 and 234 Hz.

Selfdestruction of the Mk II by the explosive charge located inside the set. Activate the friction strip through the explosive match head and quickly vacate the area. The charge will explode ten seconds latter...If possible, proceed to also destroy the battery pack and antennas. *(Practical guide for the operation of the Eureka Mk II,* dated 16 May 1944, fonds Rivière Archives du centre d'histoire et de la déportation in Lyons, France)

Below.
Eureka Mk II with its Type 304A antenna.

Country: United Kingdom
Organisation: SOE, SIS, RAF, airborne units
Manufacturer: Cossor
Introduction: 1943
Power output: 10 W
Emission and reception Frequency Bands: 213,5 MHz

This new set answered the needs of Résistance movements that required a set which could be quickly assembled and operated and which had to be lighter and smaller than the previous ones in order to be easily concealed.

The Mk III could operate on five channels while the Mk III B only had two. The Mk III was not fitted with an explosive charge for an emergency selfdestruction. The standard operating procedure was to use a CLAM magnetic charge fitted with a ten-second pencil detonator. The CLAM was to be positioned on top of the transceiver, then the assembly was to be put on the power pack; then, the copper section of the tube of the time pencil had to be crushed in order to to break the vial of cupric chloride which then would slowly eat through the wire holding back the striker...

Above.
Eureka Mk III.

Left.
**A folded Eureka
Mk III antenna.**
*(Norwegian Armed Forces
Museum Oslo, Norway)*

Next page.
**On 14 July 44, André Lacourt
a.k.a « Joseph », who had
been recruted in France
in early 1942, operates
a Eureka Mk III B during
Operation « Cadillac »
on DZ « Taille-Crayon »
(pencil sharpener) located
in Vassieux en Vercors. On
that day, 72 B17 dropped
862 containers.**
(EMA)

Emitter/Receiver
height: 19 cm
length: 7 cm
width: 10,5 cm
weight: 1,3 kg

TYPE TR 3563
Power source
height: 19 cm
length: 7 cm
width: 10,5 cm
weight: 2,1 kg

TYPE 515/515 A
Transit case
height: 30 cm
length: 20 cm
width: 48 cm

TYPE 108
Length of the antenna
(vertical on tripod): 2.7 m
Mk III: 6 volts, 30 Ah capable of 9 hours of operation.
Mk III Am: 6 volts, 30 Ah capable of roughly 7 hours of operation.
Mk III B: 6 volts, 30 Ah capable of roughly 9 hours of operation.

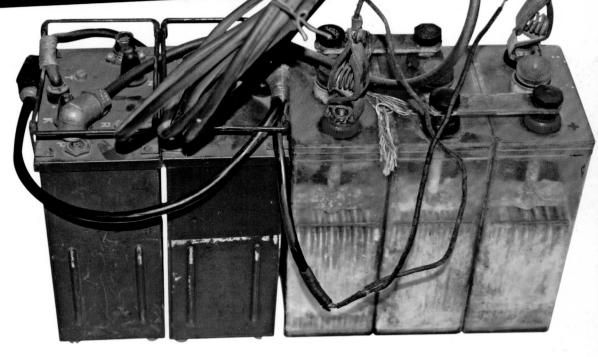

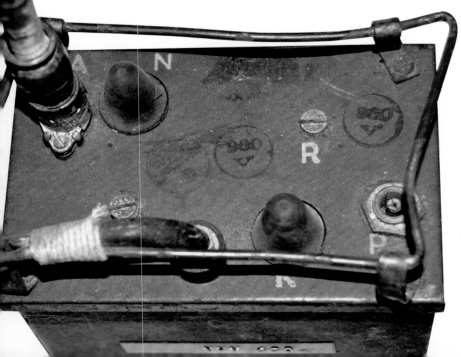

Top.
Eureka Mk III batteries.

Above.
Cable lug of a Eureka Mk III
with « Made in England » markings.

Left.
View of the top of the casing of a Eureka Mk III.
(Norwegian Armed Forces Museum collection, Oslo, Norway)

Previous page.
French historian of the SOE and of the Résitance Pierre
Lorrain and his friend Jacques Dubois re-enacting the
joint use of an S-Phone and a Eureka
(Georges Ducreuzet collection)

BIBLIOGRAPHY

- *Les ailes de la mort,* editions du Siècle, J. Mortane.
- *Missions Spéciales — La guerre des ailes,* Jacques Mortane, editions Baudinière, 1933.
- *SOE in France,* by M.R.D. Foot, Her Majesty's Stationery Office (London), 1966.
- *Missions secrètes en France,* Peter Churchill, Presses de la Cité, 1967.
- *Mettez l'Europe à feu: E.H. Cookridge, Fayard, 1968,* E.H. Cookridge, Fayard, 1968.
- Livre d'or de l'amicale des réseaux actions.
- *Parsifal, un chirurgien anglais dans le maquis de l'Ain,* Geoffrey Parker, Flammarion, 1970.
- *Histoire mondiale des parachutistes,* Pierre Sergent, editions S.P.L, 1974.
- *Armement clandestin, France 1941-1944,* Pierre Lorain, Plon 1974.
- *Assault from the Sky: History of Airborne Warfare,* John Weeks, Westbridge books, 1978.
- *CLASSE 38, Souvenirs d'un Chasseur Ardennais devenu agent parachutiste,* Adolphe Lheureux, Louis Musin editeur Bruxelles, 1979.
- *Mes missions au clair de lune. Un du S.R. Air en action,* Robert Masson, edition Pensée Moderne, 1975.
- *Un Anglais dans le maquis,* George Millar, rééd. Cêtre, 1984.
- *Les réseaux Actions de la France Combattante,* Amicale des réseaux Actions de la France Combattante, editions France Empire, 1986.
- *Nous atterrissions de nuit…,* Hugh Verity, éditions France Empire, 1986.
- *Aviateurs et Résistants,* tomes 1 à 5, revue Icare nº 141,144, 148, 151 et 153.
- *Entre lac et montagnes du Chablais,* print in Swiss Monfort SA, 1994.
- *« Pauline », Parachutée en 1943,* Pearl Cornioley, editions Par exemple, 1996.
- *Le parfait espion,* H. Keith Melton, edition N.1, 1996.
- *Triple jeu, l'espion Déricourt,* Jean Lartéguy and Bob Maloubier, Robert Laffont, 1992.
- *La girafe a un long cou,* Jacques R.E. Poirier, Fanlac, 1992.
- *La lune est pleine d'éléphants verts. Histoire des messages de Radio-Londres à la Résistance française (1942-1944),* Dominique Decèze, J. Lanzmann & Seghers editeurs, 1979.
- *L'Espoir des Ténèbres (Histoire du BOA). Parachutages sous l'Occupation,* Michel Pichard, editions Erti.
- *L'Arche de Noé, Réseau « Alliance » 1940-1945,* Marie-Madeleine Fourcade, Plon, 1998.
- *Beaulieu: The Finishing School for Secret Agents,* C. Cunningham, Leo Cooper, 1998.
- *Missions secrètes et Déportation 1939-1945–Les Roses de Picardie,* editions Heimdal, 1998.
- *Journal d'un Béké* tomes 2 et 3, Louis de Lucy de Fossarieu, Indo editions, 1999.
- *For King and Country: British Airborne Uniforms, Insignia & Equipment in World War II,* Glenn Harlan, Schiffer Publishing, 1999.
- *Secret agent: the true story of the Special Operations Executive,* David Stafford, BBC Worldwide (London, England), 2000.
- *The Secret History of SOE – Special Operations Executive 1940–1945,* William Mackenzie, St Ermin's Press, 2000.
- *Secret Agent's Handbook of Special Devices,* Public Record Office, 2000.
- *Lysander… « L'avion qui venait de Londres » De la tourmente au clair de lune,* Jean-Michel Legrand, éditions Vario, 2000.
- *Flottilles secrètes. Les liaisons clandestines en France et en Afrique du Nord, 1940-1944,* Sir Brooks Richards, Éditions Marcel-Didier Vrac, 2001.
- *SOE Syllabus: Lessons in ungentlemanly warfare, World War II,* Denis Rigden, Public Record Office, 2001.
- *La Gestapo m'appelait la souris blanche — Une Australienne au secours de la France,* Nancy Wake, editions du Félin, 2001.
- *Secret War: A Pictorial Record of the Special Operations Executive,* Juliette Pattinson, Caxton Editions, 2001.
- *World War II Troop Type Parachutes Allies: U.S., Britain, Russia,* Guy Richards, Schiffer Publishing, 2003.
- *Station 12: Aston House — SOE's Secret Centre,* Des Turner, Sutton Publishing, 2006.
- *Spies, Supplies and Moonlit Skies, Vol. II: The French Connection, April-June 1944: Code Name Neptune,* Thomas L. Ensminger, 2004.
- *Paras britanniques, Les unités, l'équipement et les opérations des « Red Devils »,* Olivier Richard, éditions ETAI.
- *Livre d'Or du Mémorial de Ramatuelle 1939-1945,* Marie Gatard, A.A.S.S.D.N.
- *Souvenirs (Tomes 1, 2 et 3),* André Dewavrin dit le colonel « Passy », éditeur Raoul Solar, 1948.

SOURCES

• BCRA, Note 644/F.F. dated 23 june 1942.
• BCRA, Memo on Pick-up and parachute operations in occupied France dated 13 August 1942.
• French Air Ministry: technical manual on the Rebecca – Eureka sets.
• BCRA (Bloc OP, MP/PA, 4ᵉ bureau) memo n ° 374 dated 10 march 1944.
• BCRA Eureka Mk III B technical manual dated 6 may 1944.
• Course notes taken by Capitaine Jean Souquet a.k.a « Carnavon » in 1944 à Milton Hall (Jedburgh).
• Procedures for para drops in the Haute-Savoie.
• BCRA, memo dated 26 May 1944 to « Marquis » (Rivière) about the setting up of an Eureka beacon codenamed « Margatte ».
• Development of technique of dropping troops and military supplies by parachute 1939-1945, Airborne Force Experimental Establishment (28 February 1949).
• Parachute experiments, source: SHD/Département Air.

PRESS ARTICLES

• *S.O.E le cheval de Troie de Sa Majesté, armement clandestin de la Résistance,*
Gazette des armes (n° 17, 18 et 33 en juin et juillet 1974, décembre 1975);
• *La tenue de saut des agents du S.O.E,* René Smeets, A.M.I. n° 6.

Author's articles:
• *La dague de l'OSS,* Militaria Magazine n° 260 march 2007
• *La dague de l'USMC,* Militaria Magazine n° 265 august 2007
• *Tenue de saut des agents alliés parachutés 1/2,* Militaria Magazine n° 273 april 2008
• *Tenue de saut des agents alliés parachutés 2/2,* Militaria Magazine n° 275 june 2008
• *Tenue précoce des agents alliés parachutés,* Militaria Magazine n° 280 november 2008
• *SAS, le PM Patchett du lieutenant Denys Cochin,* Militaria Magazine n° 318 january 2012

ACKNOWLEDGEMENTS

The author wishes to thank wholeheartedly the veterans who gave him the honour and pleasure of sharing their memories with him:
• Edgar Tupet Thomé, from the BCRA, parachuted during the night of the 9th December 1941 close to the ferme des Lagnys, 15 km South of Vatan, Châteauroux;
• Daniel Cordier « Bip-W » from the BCRA parachuted on 26 July 1942 near Coursages, 10 km South West from Montluçon;
• Marcel Jaurent-Singer radio operator of the SOE F Mason network parachuted on 3 March 1944 near Renaison, 12 km South East of Roanne;
• Général Michel Barthelemy a.k.a « Hauteur » from the BCRA landed by Hudson pick-up during the night of the 3rd to the 4th May 1944 on the "Aigle" field near Manziat, 3 km North East of Macon (Operation *Halberd*);
• Jean Guyomard from the Sussex network, parachuted during the night of the 10th to the 11th of May 1944 near Nauffles Risles in the Eure département (mission Ney) and on the 7th of July 1944 near Fouilleuse in the Oise département (Helène mission);
• Jean-Michel Rémy parachuted in May 1944 near the Othe forest in the Aube département, arrested on 27 August, escaped from the Nancy prison on 1st September 1944;
• Delmar Calvert from the Justine OSS OG parachuted on 29 June 1944 at 0h10 on DZ "Taille-crayon" (Pencil sharpener) in Vassieux-en-Vercors;
• Jean Sassi, radio operator of the « Chloroform » Jedburgh team parachuted on 30 June 1944 on the "Framboise" (Rasberry) DZ in Dieulefit (Drôme) and then, for the « Vega » mission, dropped in Mong Gnam, North Laos (Méo Country) on 4 June 1945;
• Josianne Sommers a.k.a « Venitien » radio operator of the BCRA parachuted on 7 July 1944 on DZ « Négus »;
• François Chatelin from the BCRA extracted by Lysander Pick-up during operation « Jeanette » during the night of the 13th to the 14th of May 1943 on the "Planète" field, 2 km West of Luzillé South East of Tours and then parachuted on18 July 1944 on the Poët-Laval plain in Dieulefit (Drôme);
• John Bodnard & Jack Risler, US Marines belonging to the OSS, mission Union II, parachuted on 1st August 1944 on DZ "Ebonite" on the Saisies pass (Savoie département);
• Aldo Bocconne, Aimé Flaba, Georges Ricard and Rodolphe Rossi from mission Kay II, parachuted on 20 October 1945 in Lakhom, Siam, close to Thakhek (Laos).

ACKNOWLEDGEMENTS

To the experienced collectors and faithful friends who helped me in my researches:
- The Norwegian Armed Forces Museum to Oslo, especially its curator Colonel Stein Aasland *(http://www.mil.no/felles/fmu/ start/museet/English)* the author of a very thoroughly researched and highly sought after book: « BBC: "KANONEN SILLER CHOPIN »;
- The Norway's Resistance Museum in Oslo and its curator Ivar Kraglund *(www.nhm.mil.no);*
- Nathalie Genet-Rouffiac, curator of the SHD (Military Archives Center in France).
- Colonel Debrun, president of the Amicale des Anciens des Services Spéciaux de la Défense Nationale *http://www.aassdn.org/;*
- Mr Ivar Kraglund curator of the Oslo Resistance Museum *(Norges Hjemmefrontmuseum, http://www.nhm.mil.no);*
- Thomas L. Ensminger, American author and historian of the 801st/492nd BG of the 8th AF, USAAF *http://home.comcast.net/~801492bg.historian/Index.html;*
- Vladimir Trouplin, curator of the Musée de l'Ordre de la Libération, in Paris, France *www.ordredelaliberation.fr;*
- Archives du Centre d'Histoire de la Résistance et de la Déportation, Lyons, France *www.chrd.lyon.fr;*
- Dominique Soulier, curator of the musée Sussex, Hochfelden, France *http://www.plan-sussex-1944.net/;*
- Bertrand Souquet, son and historian of the Jedburghs;
- Bruno Barthelot, Patrick Blain, Philippe Chapillon, Georges Ducreuzet, Patrick Giraud, Alain Gosselin, Laurent Jacquet, Eric Klammerek, Serge Larcher, Emmanuel Lefebvre, Magali Masselin, Philippe Mouret, Eric Pierret, Joachim Pol et Charly Roussel;
- And last but not least, Eric Micheletti for his unfaltering support!

IN THE SAME COLLECTION

LES OPÉRATEURS RADIO CLANDESTINS
ISBN : 978-2-35250-182-4

THE CLANDESTINE RADIO OPERATORS
ISBN: 978-2-35250-183-1

COMING SOON

THE BCRA, by Pascal Le Pautremat
THE SUSSEX PLAN, by Dominique Soulier
CLANDESTINE PARACHUTE AND PICK-UP OPERATIONS Volume 2, by Jean-Louis Perquin

THIS BOOK WAS EDITED BY ERIC MICHELETTI.
DESIGN AND LAYOUT MATTHIEU PLEISSINGER. CORRECTION PERRINE ROSSET. TRANSLATED BY VALERIE CAPO.
PROFILES REALISED BY NICOLAS GOHIN.

Histoire & Collections

SA au capital de 182 938,82 €
5, avenue de la République
F-75541 Paris Cédex 11—FRANCE
Tel: +33-1 40 21 18 20 / Fax: +33-1 47 00 51 11
www.histoireetcollections.com

This book has been designed, typed, laid-out and processed by *Histoire & Collections* on fully integrated computer equipment.
Color separation: Studio A&C
Print by Calidad Grafica,
Spain, European Union.
August 2012